Good Nonsense

Good Nonsense

A Body in Motion and
A Mind at Play

Sarah Austin Casson

DAIR

Book Design by Sarah Lahay

First Edition 2024

ISBN: 979-8-218-35628-6 (ebook)
ISBN: 979-8-218-35627-9 (paperback)

Library of Congress Control Number: 2024900845

Published by Dair Press
Berkeley, California
www.DairPress.com

Dair Press
A publishing company founded on intellectual curiosity and a sense of adventure.

For Sam

*He who lovingly reminds me to adventure, to dare,
and to dream—even if I'm feeling scared.
Which is to say, he who sees me as I am.*

Contents

Introduction

Running brings me joy. I am gentler on the world after a run. Hiking lets me wander, both physically and mentally. Scuba diving in deep, cold waters relaxes me. I float past cute sharks, flamboyant nudibranchs, and dying coral.

I feel almost indistinguishable from that salty water that covers 71 percent of this planet and is nearly identical to my own blood. Frequently, I lie in my purple sun-bleached hammock, which I set up between two rusty poles in the parking lot outside my apartment in Los Angeles. There I sway to my own rhythm and think about nothing—and everything.

For me, running, hiking, and diving are play. But engaged play. They allow my mind to wander in different ways over the kinds of questions that all of us find popping up in our lives. Am I enough of a runner? A hiker? A diver? What is enough? How are my own actions harming others and the planet? How do we do systemic change? How do I catch my breath, move forward with kindness, and not flail about in place? Why do I care so much? Why should I care? How do I not drown with this caring?

I like asking questions. I'm an environmental anthropologist, a scientist who situates herself in the places where nature and culture intersect. I look at difficult questions: I've worked in climate change research, the archaeology of collapsed prehistoric civilizations, and wilderness conservation policy.

Anthropology, philosophy, and stars help me ask questions. Anthropology looks at the many ways of being a human in the world. Philosophy studies ideas.

And stars? Well, stars are pretty. I simply look at them, letting myself feel awe. When you pay attention, awe shows up in most things.

So this is a book about those hard questions. And about play, which is paradoxically the best way to deal with them. These questions come unbidden to all of us. They don't care if you don't like to wrestle with hard questions in your off-duty hours, as I do. They find all of us.

You can't get away from hard questions. They arise when they want—usually when you're doing something else. After my morning run, I'll make a smoothie for second breakfast. I drop a banana into the blender, and the horrors of Dole Corporation violence float through my head. I add in frozen strawberries and wonder who picked them and if they're part of the large contingent of agricultural workers whose rights are abused. I add in heaping teaspoons of hemp protein powder, wondering about who now profits from the plant's legalization and conversion into a wellness product.

Each food comes with context and a footprint. My blender itself is a plastic derived from petroleum. My vegan smoothie overflows with environmental degradation and human injustice.

I understand why people don't enjoy asking hard questions. Even something like the sunscreen I sometimes wear as I play outside can end up feeling like a lost cause. Sunscreen is just one example of the mundane choices we make every day to protect our health. But if you think about it too much, you'll end up in a paralyzed state of dread and horror about the planet. These mundane rabbit holes can leave you feeling powerless.

When I choose to wear sunscreen, it's the reef-safe type. I do this even for nonaquatic adventures. I know reef-safe sunscreen alone will not save the reefs. These are large, complex systemic problems. No solution in isolation will be a panacea. Capitalism's solutions will not undo capitalism's problems. But, I need to wear sunscreen at times, and it feels too painful not to purchase from a brand that at least gestures towards a solution.

Many scientists are working hard to create solutions to our massive environmental problems. It's painful work that has broken many an optimistic do-gooder. Understanding the science behind the problems does not inure us to feeling the immensity of the problems.

I am on a coral scientist email listserv. They yell at one another in email missives.

One contingent reminds us all that *reef-safe* is a misnomer. It means no more than buying supposedly "natural" products at Walmart. But hey, at least reef-safe usually means the absence of two particular chemicals. That's better than nothing, yes?

No, others shout-write back. The other ingredients in sunscreen also harm reefs. We need absolute protection of our corals from sunscreen.

A third, equally depressing group on the listserv invariably pops up to ask: Does it matter? Climate change will kill all the reefs.

The argument continues around and around. The cyclical debates depress me in a comforting way. We all sweat these concepts. A single, clear answer does not exist. On the multiple-choice test of conservation and climate change, the answer is E: It all matters and none of it is wrong. That's the frustrating answer. It's not an answer.

When grief and fear overwhelm you, it can be easier to yell on the internet and point fingers. Much harder is to say quietly to yourself, "I am seeing the Great Barrier Reef die. I can barely fathom its physical size, much less the interconnected complexities of the creatures that make it the living giant that it is. I intellectually understand that it is dying. I am not sure if I can emotionally face that fact."

Like most of us, I am often afraid to look at the hard questions. It feels uncomfortable. I squirm. I might not like what I find. Have we caused irreparable damage to the planet? Will elephants be no more? How many more languages will go extinct? Questions like these have become inescapable, and the best way to deal with them is to engage them through your body itself, through movement and play.

We've forgotten so much. We prioritize so little. Play lets us reconnect.

But we don't do play so well these days. Our culture prioritizes work. We live in a digital panopticon where everything, including hobbies, becomes an opportunity for measuring, optimizing, and competing.

Even the word *recreation* itself has been industrialized. It has become a segment of the economy, more likely a government office overseeing a protected area than an actual human activity. I recently saw someone define themselves as a recreationalist. It didn't sound right. Recreation has become something we do, in our off-hours—not someone we are, not something to be done for pure enjoyment.

The *Oxford English Dictionary* defines recreation as "an activity or pastime which is pursued for the pleasure or interest it provides." That sounds pretty good—and accurate—to me. It is personal, not a bureaucratic branch of government, not commodified.

It's like the word *leisure.* It conjures up images of wine spritzers and retail therapy—silly but probably an enjoyable relaxation. We define leisure as "freedom provided by the cessation of activities" (*Merriam-Webster*). It is the ability to float along in just being, rather than the need to do something.

A life of leisure is different. Weirdly the term takes on a very different connotation from leisure as a noun. Leisure seems to be understood as a positive in our culture. In contrast, a life of leisure connotes laziness, slothfulness, and a moneyed indulgence to be judged harshly.

I think we need more of the adjectival form of the word: to do something in a *leisurely* way. In that way, a life of leisure can be a state of being. It becomes a mindset you inhabit, spent in moments of relaxed action.

What do I mean by leisure? In some cases I do mean lying in a hammock, doing nothing much. I also mean using my muscles, working physically hard, on a run, hike, dive, or some other adventure. What I want out of leisure isn't escape or mind-numbing distraction but rather deep engagement with the world around me.

So, what is the point of recreation or leisure? I think that question is similar to what is the point of human existence.

Fun, for its own sake, often gets looked down upon. You should be working, producing, turning that enjoyment into a profit. How can you afford not to? What are you doing with your life?

The correct answer to that last question never seems to be enjoying myself, engaging with life. The question *What do you do?* always irks me. Do you mean for profit? For enjoyment? How I spend my hours? I tend to be vague in my answers. Not to piss people off, but rather because I don't know how to answer. To give a short answer to *What do you do?* feels reductive of my existence—and the existence of the question-asker.

The question-asker doesn't mean to provoke an existential crisis, I understand this. But there it is.

My brain doesn't think in short quips. It goes off on tangents, gets tangled, and wanders. Fitting myself into any one box has never worked well. I'm pretty sure I put down a different potential major on almost every college application I wrote—everything from Math to International Relations. What box do you check when everything seems interesting? What answer do you give when your brain spends the day thinking about a whole lot of different things? When you pull a thread and it tugs at the entirety of the universe? *But, what is that you do again?* I don't know—exist as a human?

That question traps us in a binary of work and life. Of doing or being. And yet, life is both doing and being. We've neglected the second half. That half is a large part of what this book is about.

My favorite model for asking questions comes from the British scholar Sara Ahmed, who has a theory she calls "sweaty concepts." Ahmed has long worked for feminist solidarity inside and outside of academia, writing about how one can live an engaged life in a world that so often looks to silence women. Sweaty concepts, she believes, are the ones that irk you, that make you sweat as you work to wrap your head around them.

Sweaty concepts live in the body, requiring mental and physical effort to understand. You never quite finish answering the questions posed by such concepts. As with Montaigne writing his essays, these sweaty concept type of questions only beget more questions. The closer you get to a semblance of an answer, the more questions arise. If a sweaty concept's question is answered with something quick and tidy, it's likely untrue. We all know when something rings hollow. Sweat creates a mess.

Theory is always bodily, Ahmed argues. We think with our bodies. How we physically engage with the world directs our thoughts. Theory is not limited to the brains of dead white men. We all get to play with hard thoughts.

Sweaty concepts and the questions they ask make you exert yourself. Physical and intellectual sweating go together. These questions don't come when called. They lurk everywhere. The ephemeral yet seemingly everywhere nature of these questions frustrates me. I often sweat when frustrated. I sweat to feel un-frustrated. Moving my body calms my mind. Any movement will do. Some, like running, hiking, or diving, I prefer.

I don't have answers. I have hunches. I have ideas about the direction in which answers might lie. It's like looking for the end of the rainbow—it doesn't exist, but the rainbow is still pretty.

We shouldn't expect quick, straightforward answers to complex problems. Reality doesn't work like that. I wish it did. We like those types of quick answers, don't we?

But it's hard to think about things with any kind of nuance—or patience for someone asking for nuance—when you're burned out and scared. Almost every problem we're trying to tackle as a society (climate change, land degradation, pollution, income inequality, racial injustice, everything) can easily fall into this emergency mindset trap. Understandably so! People are dying. Whales are dying. Plastic can be found in falling snow. It all seems so overwhelming.

To a large extent, it is. Stuck in our emergency mindset, we don't have time for details.

If all you're doing is drowning, that helps no one. Happiness helps more. Not blinded, head-in-the-sand happiness that ignores cruelty and injustice. No, I mean engaged joy. A joy that can feel the hurt and still play.

We too often mistakenly try to solve sweaty concepts the same way we do everything: We see a nail and so we hammer. Sweaty concepts don't respond to hammering. They don't respond to a work-like focus. They stick around, making us feel anxious. What do they respond to? They respond to play. To physical sweat.

The Passion Paradox, by sports science writers Brad Stulberg and Steve Magness, touches on mistakenly taking the wrong approach: When passion goes bad, you dope, you cheat, you lose sight of the bigger picture. You become narrow-minded, rigid, brittle—and egotistical. You lose enjoyment.

Ask the wrong questions and you'll get the wrong answers. Look for a quick fix and you'll find it. It won't soothe your fear, though. It won't answer the questions. You'll still end up where I've been: burned out, with a hurt IT band and a fractured tibia.

Bad stress is really harmful. We know the terrible physical and mental ailments caused by suffering. But it isn't the only type of stress. We also know about the wonderful benefits of exerting yourself. In their books, Brad and Steve talk about this, using it to form a central part of their iconic equation: stress + rest = growth.

I think there's a similar equation to how we engage with the sweaty concepts of the world: sweat + play = good nonsense.

What do I mean by good nonsense? It's a little bit like John Lewis's *good trouble*, though it didn't arise out of that. I mean understanding that the best trails never follow straight lines. Life doesn't either. The most fun, the good nonsense, isn't a clear path of heavy-handed focus. It's a light-hearted meander, affording the opportunity to both smell the flowers and let hard questions flow through your mind and body as you play.

I look to good nonsense for times when my mind and body can wrestle with hard questions, when I can think my own thoughts. Real attention requires muscled effort. Physical and intellectual sweating go together for me.

During play, we can handle the questions that arise in an organic, benign manner, which is much more satisfying than ignoring or denying them. This is engaged play. You can have fun in the moment. You can goof around.

Environmental psychologists Rachel and Stephen Kaplan call this state of mind "soft fascination," when our attention is held just enough to then free our brains to explore widely, ultimately giving us a feeling of profound restoration. Time spent in nature creates the ideal setup for soft fascination. Couple that with gentle physical activity, be it a methodical hike, a wandering run, or a floating dive, and you've got an ideal situation for turning pondering into a key part of play.

We don't solve wicked problems—or make ourselves happier—by putting our heads down and pushing harder. We need a break. Working with hard questions can be a form of play, but only when we do it with a light touch. Ideas arise. You can't go get them.

We need to collectively step back, begin playing while asking a lot of hard questions with complicated answers. It is in those times when our crises seem the worst that we most need the right type of break. We need those questions. To be a tad hyperbolic: Our very existence as a species requires us to engage in good nonsense.

Life is always about to get more topsy-turvy. We need to remember to value fun. Enjoyment does not exclude a little sweat. Often, I find, they complement each other well.

So this is a book about good nonsense. It is both a personal narrative and an exploration of themes I find important to our collective understanding of our relationship to the natural world.

To play with these themes, I've organized the book into three parts, each dedicated to one of my favorite modes of good nonsense: Walking, Floating, and Running. We think not just with our brains but with our bodies. How and where you move your body can direct the texture of your thoughts. Perhaps it is because that body and its perspectives are so subjective. Subjectivity is messy, and we tend to clean up messes and sanitize them. But sometimes you need to quietly hold space for the mess.

That's where a beautiful walk—and the purposefully slow movements of the walk—help. It's hard for me to be too wound up while walking. Everything flows. Walking is linear. It leads to more methodical thoughts. The thoughts plod along, mimicking my footsteps.

When I float beneath the ocean's surface on a scuba dive, the fluidity of my movements drift my thoughts along. The otherworldliness of the marine world lends itself to creating alternative ways of viewing things. Thoughts meander along as I slowly move my body through the water's dense texture.

My attention skips about when I'm running. A bird's squawk might grab it. Or, I let myself forget where I am and disappear into thinking. That's the beauty of running—it's so rapidly repetitive and somewhat bouncy that you don't really have to pay attention to anything except what you want to notice. Disconnected ideas can collide into one another, bringing new perspectives and adventurous ideas.

That's part of all of this: adventure. When I'm at play, I want to be out there. Out where it is so beautiful, I am stunned. Where I have to work physically hard for many days to start to get there. And then keep going. I want to be somewhere remote. In the desert. In a faraway jungle. Deep underwater breathing Nitrox-infused air.

It is in those (mostly) wild places, moving my body, that I most enjoy thinking.

I don't know where my brain goes on runs, hikes, dives, or other forms of play in the outdoors. The thoughts meander and skip around. Sometimes they disappear altogether, only to appear suddenly and bounce into one another. They collide. Scatter. Loop. They blur into one another.

What I do know is that I'm kinder and more creative when I am happy. And I'm happier when my life overflows with adventure. Sunlight and sandy beaches legitimately make me a better human. So do narrow paths across high-altitude mountains, dives deep underwater, and my daily run in urban wildernesses around Los Angeles.

Like I've said: I have questions that beget more questions, and I have a few hunches. As Sara Ahmed would say, I have a sweaty concept. Fun has too often become another thing on the to-do list, something to be commodified for Instagram, done for bragging rights, an achievement in the past tense. We seem to have forgotten how to recreate for the pure joy of it. That seems a little silly: Life just isn't that serious. Play holds the key to the hardest, biggest questions of our lives.

Part I

WALK

Chapter 1

Bracketing in Borneo

I fell in love with adventures through books as a kid. I didn't chat on AIM in middle and high school except occasionally with one or two friends. Instead, I read. With books I climbed mountains, wandered deserts, and met sea creatures.

Borneo was one of the first places I can remember falling in love with through my adventure books. The Strand Bookstore near Union Station gave me my first glimpse of that forested island. Starting in sixth grade, I'd make frequent trips to that famous bookstore with one of my best friends, Sophia, taking the train into Manhattan from our tiny village, Croton-on-Hudson. We'd rummage through the severely discounted books lining the sidewalk around The Strand. There I bought a $1 used book that talked about orangutans, tall trees, and Dayak people protecting their way of life. I was hooked and wanted to know everything I could about this seemingly faraway place. I itched to get myself there. I've felt that way about the entire world for as long as I can remember. Learning about Borneo only intensified that desire.

I found more books on Borneo and located it in old atlases. It seemed to be a large splotch of dark green on the other side of the world. Books slowly gave me more context: Borneo is the second-largest rainforest and the third-biggest island in the world. The land is politically divided between Indonesia, Malaysia, and Brunei. It has high mountain peaks, like Mount Kinabalu, low peat swamp forests, and thick rainforests. Today its inhabitants live in dense modern cities, rural agricultural villages, and transient jungle camps.

Borneo books took me on long hikes through the muddy jungle. We worried about tigers and rhinoceroses and marveled at the long tongues of sun bears, the relative tininess of Borneo pygmy elephants, and the mysterious spots of clouded leopards. The authors and I got lost, hungry, and tired. We got found, too—usually with the help of those who lived in the forest and were slightly confused as to why we were exerting ourselves so hard, so seemingly unadjusted to jungle life, for the purpose of recreation.

We all do this to some degree when we read. I think that's often the point of reading: to go on someone else's adventure, to inhabit someone else's life, to remember just how big and complex our world is—and other people's inner lives who inhabit this world with us.

Do you really need to know about sun bears? Well, no. Is it enjoyable? Yes. Does thinking about how someone else might perceive an adventurous hike—be they a British ex-military man looking to prove he's still tough or a Dayak woman living deep in the jungle—help you think about others' experiences and expand empathy? Yes. Reading can't help but give us a more nuanced perspective of the world.

I wonder: Does reading about someone else's adventure count as a type of adventure?

One of the best examples I can think of to get at an answer to this question comes from an adventure book situated in an environment the exact opposite of Borneo: the Norwegian winter Arctic. Originally published in German in 1938, *A Woman in the Polar Night* tells of Christiane Ritter's time spent overwintering in the Norwegian arctic wilderness. Trained as a painter, Ritter uses beautiful language to bring you along with her and see the beauty in the mundane.

She writes, "It is a beautiful, still, and holy night, earth and sky shadowed in a tender cobalt blue. The frozen slopes of the mountains and the coast have no reality; they are a dream lit up by the soft and hazy yellow light of the sun's reflection as it moves round the northern horizon. And over everything the calm that elsewhere inheres only the world beyond our own." With Ritter, you watch her surroundings, her life—in the frequent mundane moments and the occasional worrisome ones, like the dwindling quantity of the coming months' food supplies.

I know I did not go to the twentieth-century Arctic but am sure I went somewhere when reading Ritter's work. That's the magic of reading. These days I visit (in person) lots of somewheres—and many *oh shit that's the middle of nowhere* places. I guess these wilderness adventures are more real than my childhood daydreams. But I'm honestly not so sure.

The feeling that hooked me when I first read about Borneo is what turned me into a scientist. I've been affiliated with long-running university research sites, joined one-off projects as a research assistant, conducted my own research with others working for me, and probably a few other types of field research gigs I'm forgetting about. When I'm in a wilderness area for play, I'm usually as remote as possible, relaxed, and not carrying that much. There's something distinctively different about being in a wilderness for work. There's a rush to all research. You can always gather more, better data. Grants allow for only a certain amount of time in the field. Dry seasons end. With the exception of one group of Australian archaeologists I worked with in Cambodia, I've never seen a relaxed, calm researcher in the field.

When I went to Borneo it lived up to my childhood daydreams. I wanted to come back. I wanted to find the biggest hike I could. So I did.

I brought Sam with me. He's my partner and frequent adventure buddy. We've been together since we were nineteen and met in our college dining hall. That first lunch was spent making each other laugh and discussing books—and it's basically been that way ever since. Sam prefers ocean, city, and food-oriented adventures. But, if I really want us to go on a jungle trek, he'll deal with the humidity and abundance of insects to join me.

This particular hike was the multi-week Cross Borneo Trek. It's a hike east to west across Borneo (Balikpapan to Pontianak) by foot and boat through some of the most remote jungled landscapes in the world.

Hiking as a way of travel is purposely slow. You can't really hurry a hike. Your pack is too heavy. Your boots too slow. Sure, there's fast packing but even that is a snail's pace compared to cycling or even trail running. One chooses hiking for the pacing it provides through a landscape—and its ability to traverse landscape inaccessible to faster paces. Thoughts slow to the rhythm of your footsteps. Details otherwise rushed over become a day's highlights. You may not know where the day's trail will lead but you can spend time in the immediacy of now, slowly plodding through the present moment. A long-distance hike lasts many days, usually even many weeks. You get to play in the slow, rhythmic focus of the present for days on end.

If you ever watched the *Magic School Bus* episode on dinosaurs as a kid, you (almost) know what it's like to be in a jungle: Thick, gigantic trees. Green on top of green. Ordinary plants that are supersized. Plants you've never imagined could exist, with their colors and odd shapes, grow on top of and in between other plants. The only thing missing from a real jungle is the dinosaurs, though I guess all the birds, chirping and shouting, are the remnants of those dinosaurs, just not as large.

Jungles today are filled with huge mammals and reptiles—they just know how to hide until they want to be seen. It's a truism that jaguars will have seen you long before you even guessed they might be accompanying you (and accompanying with some very large, sharp teeth and claws). It's also sadly true that jungles around the world, especially Borneo, are emptier than they should be. They look and sound incredibly densely populated with plants and animals—but that's a fragment of what they once were, what they should be to be a healthy ecosystem.

Still, you can feel the magic. The air is thick with humidity and smells. Things rot, things grow—all sending off scents and signals to other creatures: eat me, don't eat me, pollinate me, this is my territory, I peed here. Monkeys howl and insects scream. A jungle is not quiet. It is not still. There is a calmness in the chaos, distinct from the hectic feel of a city.

To get deep out there is to enter another world and begin learning a new part of our world. Trails do not stay open very long in a jungle. The forest grows back too quickly. Instead of a neatly cleared footpath, as we'd find in most United States national parks, there are clues of where to go next. Occasional machete notches on large trees indicate that you're still headed in the right direction. You pick your way among old trees, newly sprouting ones, fabulous orchids, a base layer of ferns, shrubs, and other such plant life.

I've gotten lost on other hikes in my life—usually when I follow what I had thought to be a trail, only to figure out that it was a well-worn animal footpath. I know only too well how easy it can be to get complacent and assume you're reading the landscape correctly. In the Borneo jungle, it's easy to imagine an opening in the trees is more than that—that it's clearly the path. Sometimes it is. Sometimes it's not.

It's best to go with those who can read the jungled landscape. I did this hike with four men: Sam, Burdan, Ata, and Bapa Sinta. Sam knows the jungle less than I do.

After I hired Burdan as a hiking guide, he hired Ata and Bapa Sinta—technically as porters. But their real job was their ability to deeply read the forest and their relationships with those living there. Both are Dayak and grew up in the jungle: Ata in West Kalimantan, Bapa Sinta in East Kalimantan. If an accident happened or we ran into other trouble, it was their deep knowledge of this specific trail and the forest and their individual social relationships that would be counted on to fix things.

Still, even with those who can read the landscape, specific next steps are not always known. The constant mystery of *Is this where to go?* slows down the hiking pace. It forces you to be deeply present, aware of the jungle and your place within it. You can't daydream, mentally transported somewhere far away. You have to look at the flora (and, if you're lucky, the fauna) that surrounds you at this exact moment.

Being in the immediate present can be a key part of good nonsense. Not always—sometimes being transported to the past or future is important. But too often we forget about where and when we actually exist: the present moment. In it, we delve deeper into our world.

This sharpened focus helps me notice more. I see bright mushrooms tucked away in muddy crevasses. Tiny red flowers. Trees with wide but shallow roots. There are shades and tones within the green leaves. I imagine the color descriptions and depth of language Christiane Ritter, as a painter, could bring to such a place. And then, noticing I'm mentally drifting away, I come back to the colorful present, searching for the next tree notch and walking in front of and behind my hiking companions as we generally select the same routes between these notches.

The first few days of the Cross Borneo Trek were spent on boats heading up the Mahakam River deeper into the jungle. There I read George Eliot's *Middlemarch* on my Kindle, transporting myself between England and Indonesia. Book magic works for adults, too. I'd been meaning to read the book forever and being stuck on boats for days seemed like an ideal time to dig into the extremely long novel.

Books provide a wonderful way to discuss sweaty concepts, regardless of space and time. We rarely discuss hard questions with our friends, opting to leave the questions tossing around in our heads. Books let us chat. They introduce new concepts, interrogate our ideas, and give us a slow-rolling conversation. Their ideas mix together in my head and show up as questions and quotes in my notebooks. Books provide companionship as we face hard questions. We explore jungles and visit the Arctic with books—and they come with us on our trips, making our lives richer.

Sara Ahmed calls her favorite books "companion texts." Similarly, I like to think of books as wise voices we can call upon to help us re-center towards playing in good nonsense when facing hard questions. You'll find some of my favorite wise voices peppered throughout this book.

George Eliot is one such wise voice. A novelist living in nineteenth-century England, Eliot crafted some of the best literary works ever written in the English language at a time when most women couldn't participate in public life, much less be published authors. Her books are perfect for the slowly paced thoughts that arise on a hike. They're often focused on the richness of the mundane moments while also commenting on politics and the human condition.

One line from Eliot's *Middlemarch* kept bouncing in my head as we hiked in Borneo. It was: "But even while we are talking and meditating about the earth's orbit and the solar system, what we feel and adjust our movements to is the stable earth and the changing day." That's the magic of hiking. You slowly move, step by step, along the earth, grounded in the immediate now, in only the physical necessities of being a human. It also doesn't hurt that I usually choose spectacularly beautiful places to hike.

The first boat, a two-storied houseboat, offered many days and ample hours for reading. While the later boats would be smaller and tackle swooping rapids, the houseboat plotted along. At six feet, Sam was too tall to stand up straight anywhere on the boat. I thought this was quite funny. Sam did not, especially on the third continuous day on the boat.

The best seat of the houseboat was on the front deck. There, I could read *Middlemarch* in the sunlight, occasionally noticing the riverside slowly change. I've been to many jungles and so didn't think too much about the increasing jungle-ness of the passing landscape. Sam hasn't.

Sitting next to me, he had stopped reading his own Kindle and was watching the landscape. "Where are you taking us?" Sam asked, his eyes wide and his smile a tad nervous.

I looked around and noticed what he was seeing: high river cliffs, a brown river, soaring birds, screeching insects, and a jungle landscape where trees were covered in vines so thick, it looked more like a green moss wall than a forest. The river was slowly guiding us from cities to villages to remote wilderness.

It is this relationship to rivers that makes the Cross Borneo Trek distinct from other jungle hikes, even those in other areas of Borneo. It is a journey directed by water. You take boats up the Mahakam River in East Kalimantan until even the shallowest dugout canoe cannot traverse the water. Then you start walking.

The route continues with the river, following it backward up to its beginning at the highest point in the Müller Mountains. You then follow the Kapuas River downstream as you descend into West Kalimantan. A river provides a natural trail through this part of the jungle.

With rapids, waterfalls, and rushing currents, the river isn't a direct path to follow but instead a consistent gap in the forest, heading in the direction we want to go. It stays open when other gaps come and go. Rocks nestle into the silty riverbed. To get back and forth, you play a slow hopscotch with these rocks. A tricky maneuver, to be sure, but not as challenging as hiking on the sides of the river. That's where I slipped the most.

I've been on other trails in other areas of remote Borneo. On those trails I was most concerned about rotting wooden ladders, used to avoid having to scale cliffsides, potentially disintegrating as I climbed them. Here on the Cross Borneo Trek, I was concerned about the trail itself. I've never done a hike with more constant elevation gain and drop, where every step slides through slippery mud instead of staying steady where you put it, and where a misstep could have you falling down a jungled cliffside, unlikely to return.

As we slipped and carefully stepped, Burdan kept telling a story of a Dutch woman who died hiking this trail in 2011, multiple times a day. The story got more and more elaborate with each telling. I have no idea if the story was true or not. I tried to look it up in newspaper reports later but found nothing. We did pass by her gravesite at the top of a waterfall she supposedly fell down, hit her head, and died days later, awaiting helicopter rescue from the military.

It doesn't really matter whether or not Burdan's story is true. I've been in enough remote wildernesses to know that the sentiment behind the story is true: Local knowledge of a jungle—of the locations, plants, and people—can make a life or death difference.

When you get into remote wildernesses, you are re-minded just how big our planet is. There are plenty of places still left to disappear without a trace. And plenty of places where it's easy to forget the rest of the world.

Today, the world often feels small and known. It's easy to feel like we know everything there is to know and that as a global society we've mapped everywhere and discovered all the mysteries. Getting outdoors helps remind us how little we actually know.

The forest canopy in a jungle is often too thick for a helicopter to spot you from above. So in an emergency, even if we had a signal for the emergency satellite phone to call for help, the Indonesian military would not find us unless we could give them an exact location. Ata and Bapa Sinta would be the ones saving us if something happened—no military helicopter would ever reach us in time.

Almost as important was the levity each brought. A playful attitude helps make sweating through a jungle fun. Burdan had hired Ata and Bapa Sinta for their technical skills, sure. But he also knew that the two cracked the weirdest, funniest jokes. Those jokes became increasingly funny as we spent more days in the remote wilderness (as usually happens on such trips).

Ata kept shouting "MY LIIIIIIIIIIFE" in English in a bad Italian accent at odd intervals throughout our hike—often during a river crossing, as he giggled and looked up at the sky, arms spread wide. Sometimes, if he was really feeling the humor of his joke, he'd belly flop into the river. It got funnier each time he did it. As happens with many jokes repeatedly told on an adventure, saying "my liiiiiiiiiife" is still an inside joke between Sam and me.

Over time Ata explained the context of this joke: The previous year he had guided a bunch of Italian men along this trek. The Indonesian guides, including Ata, didn't speak English well—neither did the Italians. One of the Italians took himself and the spectacular nature of the jungle very seriously. So much so that every once in a while, the self-important Italian man stopped to shout "This is my life!" and then flopped himself into the river at the end of a long day's hike. Ata found this hilarious—hence his oft-repeated non-joke joke.

It also wasn't a joke that that Italian man—and myself and Sam—were recreating in an extremely poor place quite far from our own homes. Our concept of adventure was Ata's backyard. The amount of money we had paid to get ourselves to his backyard is a large amount of money in the jungle.

Ata understood this more than most of the jungle's residents we passed on the trail, many of whom he knew personally. He had left his village to earn a degree in sports science and become a gym teacher in a rapidly developing city on the other side of Borneo. After a few years the steady paycheck and allure of the big city wasn't enough, and Ata quit and returned to his jungle village life. It's a much more financially precarious lifestyle, but one in which he spends days on end in the jungle. To him, this is a much better trade-off.

Having left the jungle, Ata understood just how far we had flown to reach it—and how much those airplane tickets had cost us. Having returned, he also deeply understood just how special Borneo is and why one might go through all the trouble to get there.

So while Ata laughed at his own non-joke joke, often getting the rest of us to giggle with him, it also hinted at something much less funny: the global political power dynamics at play in most guided adventures in remote places as well as just how special the Borneo jungle is. Laughing at serious things sometimes is the best way to handle a sweaty concept. It gives us good nonsense.

We spent our days walking in and out of jungle canopy. When we were in the jungle, all I could see was dense green vegetation in myopic detail. When we crossed a river, the rest of the world would appear: the sun, the sky, the brown river with a long sight line.

This reminded me of something I've studied in the past—the idea of bracketing. To bracket is to remove everything except the experience of the thing itself. It requires you to leave out the unknowable unknowns and focus on the phenomena present. Step away from the rhetorical logic hiding wild guesses with no provable answers. Play in your experiences now. Such an approach focuses your attention on the immediate temporal and physical reality. Such limits create magic.

Edmund Husserl came up with the idea of bracketing. He was a twentieth-century German philosopher who studied how we experience consciousness. You might not recognize his name, but much of how we today talk about our existence as alive beings who see, feel, and taste our world can be traced back to his philosophy.

Christiane Ritter understood this. The starkness of the Arctic and how she chose to live there is another form of physical bracketing, I'd say. It strips away everything except what is right in front of her. It takes away everything except what she is experiencing. She wrote, "No, the Arctic does not yield its secret for the price of a ship's ticket. You must live through the long night, the storms, and the destruction of human pride. You must have gazed on the deadness of all things to grasp their livingness. In the return of light, in the magic of the ice, in the life-rhythm of the animals observed in the wilderness, in the natural laws of all being, revealed here in their completeness, lies the secret of the Arctic and the overpowering beauty of its lands." You have to *notice* the world. Ritter isn't glorifying the hardships endured but simply stating that stripped to the bareness that is winter in the Arctic, one can truly see.

Whereas Ritter had the starkness of the Arctic, I had the jungle. Vines, tree trunks, and leaves bracket out the contextual landscape. All one can see are the immediate phenomena. In a good way, I find it hard to gain perspective in a jungle. I theoretically understand, but can't see, the abundance of life in the tree canopies hundreds of feet above my head—or even around on the ground. I can hear it. Smell it.

On a treacherous hike, everything else melts away. You can forget. You can focus. You can play in the experience.

Once, at 2 a.m., the bracketing dropped completely.

You see, I had to pee and wasn't sleeping well because I was cold. For the millionth time I had forgotten that I get cold at night in jungles. I can tell you to remember to keep your dry clothes dry to prevent getting too cold. I forget to tell myself to pack for (relatively) chilly nights. I didn't bring warm clothes for sleeping or even a sleeping bag, only a silk sleeping bag liner.

Sure, this had saved me some pack weight. That seemed utterly unimportant (and a tad stupid) as I tightly wrapped myself in an extra tarp to hold in a smidge more of my body's heat. It kept in some heat, but mostly it kept in moisture. I was covered in a layer of slowly cooling sweat, which could not evaporate into the night. Getting up to go pee and to walk around and warm myself felt a much better option than lying there, cursing my forgetfulness.

I should have known better—both from my own jungle experiences and from my childhood adventure books. Those books taught me concrete adventuring techniques that I utilize today. (That is, when I don't forget to pack properly.)

In my Borneo books I learned about the importance of bringing two outfits to a jungle: one wet, one dry. Daytime brings you across rivers and along humid trails that induce profound sweating. Wet clothes take approximately forever to dry in a jungle's humidity. A trying-to-sleep, tired, sweaty body covered in those very wet, not going to dry, clothing becomes a perfect candidate for a perverse form of hypothermia: when you get dangerously too cold in a tropical rainforest. Plus, if you're wet all the time, your skin will start to rot.

When I'm deep in a jungle it feels spectacular to change out of wet socks into dry, fluffy, practically clean socks for the night. It feels revolting to do the opposite the following morning.

Usually field research means a haphazardly set-up camp in the backcountry with tents and a few cookstoves. If the research involves interviewing people, your bed might be the floor of someone's house in a remote village—maybe even a hammock, if you're lucky. Sometimes, if both the location and grant funding allow, there's a hotel room bed and a truck to drive to the field site.

On this hike we were sleeping only on a ground tarp, which I almost always prefer to a tent. Instead of a loud tent zipper, I pulled the sweaty extra tarp off myself and snuck away from the group. I peed and then walked to the river.

Husserlian bracketing created by a jungle's canopy often blocks my view of stars at night. A river provides a gap. (Deforestation does too. It's much more depressing.) At 2 a.m., bladder relieved and body still a tad cold, I sat on the edge of the riverbed and looked up. The bracketing had dropped, and I could see what seemed to be the entire universe.

I saw what seemed like a million different stars against a backdrop of black that seemingly contained all the colors. The sky had navy tones, had purple hints—and the stars weren't just white. There were yellows and reds and oranges in those twinkling dots.

We can see this richness in colors everywhere, if we let ourselves. A single color always has depth, whether you find it in a picture book, in your home garden, or in the stars above. Looking at something beautiful—and dropping our bracketing to do so—for the sake of seeing the beauty is a deep act of good nonsense.

By focusing on something like colors and allowing myself to be reminded of the specialness of the universe, I often find myself inhabiting a wider perspective on life. We can all feel a bit narrow-brained and hyper-focused at times. Sometimes it's useful, important even. (You don't get work done if you're just staring at trees, awing at the color of their leaves.) But, the reverse is also true: To see the fullness of the universe is critical for a fully inhabited life.

Ritter found ways to drop her bracketing as well: "Every now and then I take off my snow glasses to enjoy the colours of the ice. The even surfaces and gentle slopes are a light carmine red, and everything that is turned away from the sun vibrates in the celestially pure colours of the spectrum, from lilac to the deepest and purest cobalt blue."

To focus on the immediate phenomena lets us embrace where we are in life and spend time actually seeing it. It teaches us to engage with the world around us, starting with particular things. It is only through this focusing that we can begin to re-remember that everything truly is connected. To examine one thing is to examine the world.

The stars that night reminded me of what the French philosopher Maurice Merleau-Ponty argued about bracketing, that "the most important lesson which reduction teaches us is the impossibility of a complete reduction." We know the world outside the forest exists, even if we momentarily only focus on our immediate place within the jungle. You cannot truly bracket, but there's still value in the intellectual (and physical) exercise in it.

I continued to sit on the riverbed for a while longer, watching the stars. I listened to the river gurgle and giggle. Lack of ample rains made the river low that year. Water slipped over table-sized boulders and cereal-box-sized rocks. The starlight sparkled on the river's moving surface, reflecting the spectacle of the universe.

Chapter 2

Solitude in Copenhagen

It wound up taking Sam and me seventeen days to cross Borneo. We were covered in leeches, river water, and mud. Had I walked 500 feet in any direction during the hike, I would have been lost for days. I worked hard on that hike to remain un-lost. But I do value getting lost. Letting myself get physically lost is an easy way to allow my mind to wander.

I find cities to be the best places to get lost on purpose. You can just as easily get lost amid a grid of buildings and highways as in a jungle.

My agenda when I travel by myself is often no agenda. I follow my curiosity, often allowing myself to get wildly lost. That's how I found myself wandering around, slightly befuddled, in one of the most beautiful multiuse graveyards in the world: Assistents Cemetery in Copenhagen.

Cemeteries too often feel like zones of sadness, relegated to that one feeling only. Keeping the grief within a bounded area—allowing only the activity of crying, of mourning, in graveyards—lets us pretend to not have to deal with it in other locations. That isn't, of course, how feelings work. They come, they go. They blend together. You can be both happy and sad. Mournful and thankful.

That's what I appreciate about the Assistents Cemetery— that other feelings are allowed in. It's an active burial ground— people are still being added—but that's not the only use of the space. People picnic. Children laugh. Couples read books on shared blankets. Walkers meander.

At one point in its history, the Assistents Cemetery became so raucous with merriment that the government tried to ban consuming alcoholic beverages. I didn't see anyone partying that hard but wouldn't have minded it if I did. Mostly I saw people quietly enjoying themselves among the ample greenery and aging headstones.

It's a great place to get lost—and be alone, given that Denmark has a culture that doesn't do stranger small talk. The juxtaposition of life lost and life continuing to be lived creates a wonderful backdrop to let your mind wander as you physically wander.

I didn't know all this about the cemetery created in 1760 when I came across it as I walked around Copenhagen. I just thought it was a park adjacent to the street. Nørrebro, the district where I was staying, is filled with great bike paths, walking paths, hip families hanging out, delicious restaurants, cute cafes, and sweeping parks. Assistents Cemetery seemed more of the same. (It is, just with the addition of graves.)

My plan for the morning had been to wander—and meandering around Assistents fit right into that. I plan to get lost on my trips. You see, I get lost all the time anyway. So I've learned to stop fighting it and relish the unknowing instead.

That's one of the things I love about allowing myself these periods of explicit good nonsense during my travels. Travel is this distinct time when we are not fully in control and instead allow life to happen as it happens. When we wander we're in a more enjoyable, exploratory headspace.

Plus, for me at least, it's honestly just easier to let things unfold and trust that I'll be fine than to try to stay on top of my exact coordinates in a city without getting turned around.

Some people seem to always know where north is—I don't (Sam does). I only know a place after I've hiked, walked, or run it. That way I can recognize visual clues I've seen before to create a map in my head. If I pay close enough attention, I can transpose a paper map or Google Maps onto the physical reality in front of me, but that requires intense concentration. So I like to get lost on purpose, with guardrails.

The best way I've found is to give myself a few ideas of options should I want them when I arrive in a place. I do lots of research ahead of trips. I enjoy researching and imagining where I'm about to be. I find good food spots, interesting art, and whatever else I might want to visit. Then I do something I learned from Sam: Give yourself guardrails on Google Maps. Star every single one of those places, with notes if needed, into Google Maps, download the map to your phone, and then turn your phone off. Walk towards something that looks intriguing, then the next thing, and the next. Get wildly lost. Hungry? Turn your phone on and see what good food is around you. Too lost? Turn your phone on. Wanting something specific? Again, the phone.

Wandering on your own in a new city is easy, is fun. Exploration and boredom go together for me. You follow your thoughts and your own feet. You and your daydreams get to call the entire agenda. What to eat. What to see. Want to just look for good notebooks in tiny hidden shops instead of going to the supposedly amazing art museums? Yes please. (I do love museums. I love notebooks more.) Along the way, lost down backstreets, you find tasty food, odd architecture, and hidden parks that are actually cemeteries. Meandering lets me see more than I would have otherwise.

The problem with most graveyards is that you can't play in them. If I were to break out a Frisbee or a picnic blanket or lace up my running shoes and do a loop, people would think I'm being sacrilegious. It's weird that in many cities the places most full of life in terms of trees, grass, and bugs are reserved for dead people.

But Assistents is a cemetery like I'd design one. Here people were pushing carriages, babies giggled on blankets, couples strolled. At twenty-five hectares, it's a sizable amount of greenspace used by those both dead and alive. Walking around it, I stumbled upon the grave of one of the most famous walkers to live: Søren Kierkegaard, the existentialist philosopher who died in 1855 at forty-two.

He's maybe one of the most iconic anxiety-prone individuals to have lived. Kierkegaard's anxiety (and despair) was so much that he made a whole new field of philosophy from it. One of his most famous books is titled *Fear and Trembling.* Talk about lemonade from lemons.

Born to a newly wealthy family in Copenhagen, Kierkegaard was expected to continue doing what his brothers and father did: get married, attend church, maybe work for the church, and make money. He couldn't do it—his gnawing anxiety about existence and what it meant to be a religious human was too much. Instead, he took his inheritance and spent it on living expenses and publishing his writing. (He died right around the time the inherited money ran out.)

In writing that largely went ignored for a hundred years, Kierkegaard questioned the mundanity and group-think of everyday life in the sleepy Lutheran Protestant city of Copenhagen—he knew how to grapple with sweaty concepts, which, for him, were primarily religious. He created and expanded upon some of the most interesting areas of philosophy: subjective and objective truth, free will, existentialism, self, authenticity, and a lot more.

To move through his anxiety and think about his writings, Kierkegaard often walked the streets of Copenhagen. As he wrote in a letter to his depressed, hypochondriac, and bedridden niece: "Above all, do not lose your desire to walk. Everyday, I walk myself into a state of well-being & walk away from every illness. I have walked myself into my best thoughts, and I know of no thought so burdensome that one cannot walk away from it. But by sitting still, & the more one sits still, the closer one comes to feeling ill. Thus if one just keeps on walking, everything will be all right."

My concept of good nonsense echoes what Kierkegaard is saying here: You need to inhabit your body for a life well lived. While his advice might not be exactly advisable for every illness or mental disorder, Kierkegaard is spot on for the importance of inhabiting our bodies—that moving our bodies helps our minds. And, he wasn't talking from a space of abstraction or theory: His mind, with its extreme anxiety, seemed to be a hard one to inhabit.

Kierkegaard's lifetime seems so far removed from ours today that it didn't feel like I was in the same city he once lived in, much less the same cemetery where he was buried. Yet, the topics he covered and the problems he faced (and created) feel as relevant as ever to our world today.

Much of his work in his journals and published under pseudonyms and occasionally under his name features Kierkegaard existentially howling over the questions of how one should live a life. His angst is something I can relate to, in ways I'm not always the most delighted by. He was an anxious grump who thought too much about himself and his own importance to history. Example: He physically cut out pieces of his journals' pages that he didn't want read after he was dead. That requires a certain type of hubris to assume you're important enough people will want to read your diaries. To be fair, he was right: We do read them.

Kierkegaard keeps being read because he hit on something so universal. We all feel (at times) grumpy, anxious, fearful—that we've fucked everything up and everything is stupid. And he's right: Walking is sometimes the best way to move through those feelings and remember other ways of existing. Getting lost while walking gives us a momentary disorientation through which we have a better chance at a more attuned life. As Kierkegaard wrote, "To dare is to lose one's footing momentarily. Not to dare is to lose oneself."

In our own times, there's a writer named Patricia Hampl who has become one of my favorite wise voices. She's a memoirist from Minnesota who has been writing, editing, and teaching since the 1970s—along the way, she's won some pretty impressive awards: a MacArthur Fellowship, a Guggenheim Fellowship, and a bunch more. In her 2018 book, *The Art of the Wasted Day*, Hampl argues that the hours we spend mostly full of what seems to be mundane boredom are actually the most valuable. Having just lost her husband, she uses the book as an exploration of what most matters in life.

Hampl, I think, understands much of what Kierkegaard realized. She writes: "There is no language for this, not then, not even now this inner glide, articulation of the wordless, plotless truth of existence. Life is not made up of stories, much as I adore them—Charlotte, Heidi, Caddie Woodlawn. Really, life is—*this*. It's a float, my body a cloud drifting along, effortless but aware. Drifting over the world, seeing, passing along."

You exist without an agenda or a whiff of a motive. You smell the grass of the Assistents Cemetery—not because you intend to smell the grass or watch the clouds but because you're just drifting along. Leisure is when you can bounce around in your brain and remember you're on a rock hurtling through space through a galaxy that is one of many galaxies in the universe. In the next instance, you're watching a butterfly flit around, seemingly nowhere in particular. It flies away. You notice that a cloud kinda looks like a dragon. Now you're thinking about *Lord of the Rings* and how the One Ring to rule them all could be melted by dragon's fire. You start thinking about Tolkien's probably large amount of PTSD from World War I and that entire generation's trauma and the pointlessness of war and hurting one another. Then you smell the grass again and sink into that smell, drifting on to something else.

I've been to dozens of cities on my own, mostly eating my way through the new place as I wander around. It's probably the anthropologist in me, but I find the strange everyday life in a new place much more interesting than the guided route of things deemed worthy of a visit by guidebooks.

The beginning of my trips alone always feels like a stumble. For me, solitude can feel like jumping into a cold ocean. You brace for the hurt and are surprised that the whole thing feels strangely pleasant when relaxed.

Hearing yourself requires solitude. Being that brave is scary. That's one reason so many of us would rather refresh Instagram or watch TikTok than just sit in silence with our thoughts. Those apps are also purposely addictive, but that doesn't negate that we can still prefer the bland safeness of screens over the bravery required of solitude.

It's scary to give yourself solitude, demand that others respect your solitude, hear yourself in that solitude, and act on what you hear in that solitude. As the Canadian adventurer Kate Harris, who biked the Silk Road, put it in *The Land of Lost Borders*: "I felt great about my life decisions, until I felt terrified." Same, Kate, same.

I don't think there's another way to do it, to find your why, to live life adventurously, to play in good nonsense. That maybe it isn't all about getting to a point where you feel comfortable all the time. Instead it might be (as so many self-help and Buddhist books recommend) to befriend fear and learn to distinguish between the different internal screams.

Some internal screams are just looping anxiety, telling you everything is terrible, it is all ruined, why did you even bother, and why do you keep trying. Other, smarter ones go *oooooooh, this does not feel right, something is wrong here.* Learning how to distinguish between those voices—and even identifying them—takes time.

Trust me, I panic often. I've traveled by myself a lot, more than most. I still freak out every time I'm about to go on a trip alone. My brain whisper-screams that maybe this is the time when I'm not capable, and perhaps the loneliness will appear, eat me up, and I'll disintegrate. Better to stay at home. Better to avoid solitude.

I pack my bags anyway. I give that fear a cute pat on the head even though I feel like I've drunk twenty coffees on the way to the airport before a solo trip. Then something magical happens as I exit TSA. Suddenly my brain remembers: Oh, actually, I love this shit. I'm not lonely. I've got me—and every other person I might meet on my trip. (I'm much more friendly to strangers and outgoing when I travel by myself. It's a phenomenon I think many women who travel solo relate to.)

When I get past TSA I remember that the fear screaming isn't how I feel. It's just that my brain is screaming for some reason. Does this knowledge make my next trip less scary as I head to the airport? Nope. Every single time my brain becomes convinced that this is the time everything will go terribly wrong, even though that's never been the case—ever.

Once I'm in trip mode, that screaming fear rarely pops its head up again on the trip, no matter how long it is. Solitude (plus therapy) is what let me figure out that pattern in my brain. It helped me realize that sometimes I enjoy doing the things my brain would like me to think I am terrified of and should absolutely not be doing.

I'm brave and adventurous, not through an absence of fear, but because I feel that fear and do it anyway. I've never known another way of doing it. The fear screams have gotten quieter over the years as the adventures continue to stack up in numbers and complexity. The fear never goes away. It's a constant companion at the beginning of every trip.

Solitude lets me be brave. Solitude allows me to engage more fully with the world. It has never only meant sitting at home doing nothing.

Often we think in binaries: black/white, good/bad, male/female, etc. The solo travel I love so much gives us an easy binary: Alone or together? Solitude or not? Reading does the same thing. Am I chatting with the wise voices in my books or alone in a library?

But binaries can be dangerous, creating a worldview in which when we win, someone else loses. Take climate change, for example. To talk about tackling climate change is to think that we are separate from the natural world. To protect nature there must be another who destroys it. To stop climate change there must be another who continues it.

Who is this another? It is both me and someone else. I am creating climate change. You are too. I am working to stop climate change. Hopefully, so are you. These binaries squish.

You and I are separate—and together. Empathy high-lights the complications of these binaries. It comes up a lot when we think about our sweatiest concepts: poverty, climate change, inequality, etc.

When we recognize hurt in the world, we often feel it as one collective entity. If my head is drowning in other people's emotions, it feels productive—helpful even—to feel that hurt on their behalf.

But you know what I've learned? That doesn't lessen anyone else's pain. It doesn't help. We must show up for one another but not try to enmesh. Injustice doesn't disappear when you drown with another. It lessens when you do something about that inequality.

Feel distraught about climate change and injustice. (Most Americans could probably do with feeling a tad more distraught.) Don't try to take on someone else's distraught feelings. The distinction is tricky.

Others are others. I am me. We are all in this world together. I can navigate this paradox more easily when my brain isn't overloaded.

Unfairness will probably never not piss me off. I'm not trying to become a psychopath who feels nothing when she witnesses another's pain. But I know that if we all just despair, nothing will change. The change we all want to see in the world should come from joy, not fear. Otherwise we're fighting imagined enemies.

We mistake solitude for punishment. Solitude is not the same as loneliness. They're different. There can be overlap, sure. They can happen simultaneously, but that doesn't mean they're the same. It's the old correlation or causation distinction.

To be together, we need time alone. I don't think mine is the only brain that needs some solitude, especially when that time is in nature. Plenty of research points to how much happier and more creative we are when immersed in nature. Any nature—even the Assistents Cemetery—counts. I'm not arguing for solitude all the time. That sounds terrible. Hanging out with others is fun. But I think it's important to have protected pockets of time where only your brain is speaking to you.

One of my favorite thinkers about solitude is a woman named Audrey Sutherland. As a single mother she raised four children in Hawaii. Having grown up adventuring, Audrey was familiar with the outdoors when she embarked on her first expedition in 1962: a weeklong solo swim along the northeast shoreline of Molokai, towing her belongings behind her in a foam cooler box during the day and wild camping at night. That trip turned into another and another. She eventually bought a mail-ordered inflatable canoe (the better to carry her stuff) to continue exploring the Molokai waters.

Up through her eighties, Audrey continued exploring in her inflatable canoe, often for a week or more every summer. After that first solo trip, she slowly expanded the distance covered and geographical regions she canoed by herself. She'd frequent Alaska and British Columbia consistently over the years—bringing garlic, olive oil, and Hawaiian salt with her and foraging the rest of her meals.

To call her a badass is an understatement. She's often called the Queen of Adventuring Solo for a very good reason. As she wrote in *Paddling My Own Canoe*: "We rarely find out if we like having our own mind as company for days or weeks at a time. How many people have ever been totally isolated, ten miles from the nearest other human, even for two days?" We don't often get—or give ourselves—that type of quality time. It's a shame, I think. We miss out on ourselves.

Giving another person quality, device-free attention is important and a sign of respect for their thoughts and time. We owe ourselves that type of respect.

Sutherland continues: "Alone, you are more aware of surroundings, wary as an animal to danger, limp and relaxed when the sun, the brown earth, or the deep grass say, 'rest now.' Alone, you stand at night, alert, heaving poised, through ears and open mouth and fingertips. Alone, you do not worry whether someone else is tired or hungry or needing. You push yourself hard or quit for the day, reveling in the luxury of solitude. And unconcerned with human needs, you become a fish, a boulder, a tree—a part of the world around you."

Solitude gives you the luxury to do what your body asks of you. You get to exist in your own needs and rhythms. Watch yourself as you watch the world around you.

What do you think about as you eat your dinner alone? Or drink your morning coffee?

Out there, on a solo adventure, finding this solitude becomes easier once you've made the initial leap to go. But it's not just out-there solitude we need. The everyday solitude needs protection as well.

That doesn't have to be in a cave. I consider solitude a day spent working on an interesting project. Alone and together, again it's not that clear. If you're working alone remotely, it can feel like solitude. But if you're banging out emails on a stressful project, I don't think of that as solitude.

Best of all is the everyday solitude. When you're not in a conversation with anyone else—virtual, in a book, or in person.

You've got to have that here and now solitude. The space—mental and physical—to do whatever you damn well please. A space without others' thoughts or opinions, be they real or imagined.

Yet when we're alone, our self can feel crowded by other people's definitions of how a human should exist. Or, scared of others' judgments of our choice to be alone for a bit. Often solitude is not as easy as Audrey experienced it.

The imagined opinions of others can be just as restricting as real, voiced-aloud ones. Sara Maitland writes about these accusing voices in *How to Be Alone*: "I think that perhaps everyone," she writes, "is haunted by an inner ghost who undermines creativity by implying that there are better things to do with your time, asking sarcastically who you think you are and preaching modesty and humility and 'unselfishness,' or the social duty to get rich, help other people and be a good team player or other social obligations. If these are really social constructs which we have internalized, they tie very neatly into our society's negative views about solitude: the two reinforce each other."

The inner ghost that whispers, *How dare you spend time just on yourself?* It doesn't like the idea of solitude because then you can notice and hear the ghost's opinions for what they are: other people's bullshit, not your own thoughts.

The ghost's true enemy is boredom. I think without some doses of boredom, most adventures are not obtainable. To goof around in life requires the ability to luxuriate in boredom. All adventures require long stretches of doing nothing much. Anyone who cannot handle that is annoying to adventure with—at best. At worst, they do something stupid in an attempt to relieve their boredom and jeopardize the safety of everyone adventuring.

Too many are scared of boredom, of stillness, of nothingness. (Kierkegaard clearly was.) Boredom gets sold as something bad, to be avoided. I think this is a misunderstanding of the concept of boredom as well as a lost opportunity in our lives.

Boredom can feel scary because it's often the only time we can actually feel our feelings. In that pocket of boredom, if you're depressed, anxious, or uncomfortable, you will be confronted with that feeling. It bubbles up, unstopped by the usual treadmill of productivity and doing. When the not-good-enough drumbeat reaches loud-enough volumes, being bored feels the worst. It feels shameful. It feels scary.

When you luxuriate in boredom, you also can feel good. That good boredom is what the Buddhists call cool boredom— as opposed to the anxious, angsty hot boredom. Cool boredom can feel like an invitation to relax rather than a threat to your well-being.

Is it inherently necessary to think that existential thoughts are stressful? I don't think so (most of the time). I think they're pretty fun to play with—that's, honestly, the premise of my thoughts surrounding good nonsense. For that fun to appear you need large spaces of nothingness. That nothingness usually accompanies periods of comfortable, cool boredom.

Boredom isn't an escape from striving, from engaging in the world. It's fundamental to both. It lets you mentally and physically wander—to get lost.

How do you submerge yourself in cool boredom and get pleasantly lost? The first thing I do is turn off my phone. It's one of the best examples of bracketing in action. In the jungle, it's easy—the bracketing is done for me. But in a city it's harder. I have the world around me and the world in my phone. So I turn off my phone to bracket out those distractions.

I did have my phone with me in the Assistents Cemetery— you need a phone to do the Google Maps starring trick. You don't need to engage with the phone. There's tremendous power in turning off your phone. It transforms from an almost sentient creature with invisible tentacles into an odd rectangle, only notable for the number of finger smudges on it. I love it when my phone becomes a brick of extra weight at the bottom of my bag, completely forgotten about.

By the time I had walked a few blocks and stumbled onto Assistents, my lack of phone engagement had turned from hot, angsty boredom to cool boredom. That calmness continued as my wandering took me out of the cemetery and through the rest of the city. I popped into ceramic stores I might have brushed past otherwise. I meandered past elegantly designed houseboats. I ate lots of food, much of which was topped with what seemed to be local sprouts, pungent in their sprightliness. Thoughts came and went.

Boredom lets our brain make connections it usually would not. You have the mental space to mush them together. Boredom provides you the luxury to be utterly nonsensical. If your goal is to be bored, there's less of a need to be presentable, to be accountable, to be polished, or to represent yourself well. Adventure does this too.

Not just wilderness adventure. The rhythm of an urban walk lets you be wild with your thoughts, too. In a hectic city, you can pay little attention to food or shelter in ways you just can't on a wilderness hike. That frees up tremendous brain space for surprise and delight.

I often craft my urban walks to emphasize the un-expected. I want to get hopelessly lost, only to stumble upon a dish perfected over the years by this specific street vendor or restaurant chef. The food served hot and fast. I want to be surrounded by peoples, cultures, and languages I do not understand but can slowly learn more about over many visits.

During such times, I mostly exist in a state of cool boredom. When you're bored, you hear yourself in ways unattainable in a busy life. You can hear the tiny voice asking *Why?* There's a book I love about boredom, called *Boredom*. It's by a Classics professor, Peter Toohey, who teaches at the University of Calgary. He's got a great line about boredom: "It can allow you to be yourself."

I think many people don't know who their self is—or wish their self was different. Many have stuffed down some internalized, mean thoughts. Getting bored means not being able to run away from those thoughts.

Running from boredom also means avoiding the truly joyful, fun thoughts. We're often scared of those as well, huh? I think we're all a bit nervous about many things, most of which would make our lives richer, deeper, more pleasant, and joyful when faced.

Your ability to adventure depends on your skills to situate yourself in boredom. Not all the time but most of the time. Tediousness is often associated with boredom, which is a good thing. Much of adventure has profound moments of tediousness. When something is boring, you usually are stuck sitting in it. That doesn't mean you can't also enjoy it.

Adventure is sometimes deeply unenjoyable. It might be enjoyable in retrospect—we call that a Type II adventure. Some of the most fun adventures are absolute disasters and utterly not comfortable. Often, it is tedious and enjoyable. You sweat. You work. Push yourself. Giggle. Goof around. You delight in the world around you. I adventure for these delights—nothing more but also nothing less.

Adventure is a little bit like the work-life paradigm that work is always terrible and life is always good. We forget that work and life are not binary. Life is all there is.

Chapter 3

Perspective in the Nepali Himalaya

I used to think I understood how tall the Himalayan mountains were. I've spent a decent amount of time near them and on them at their lower-mid elevations in a few different countries. Lower is relative here. It still felt plenty high in the sky to me.

I knew at these lower elevations that the higher elevations of the Himalayas stretched much farther up into the sky. Duh. The lower elevations felt high, so really high up must be really, really up there.

That's how my brain conceptualized the height of the Himalayas. Just really, really high.

Did I know what these distances into the sky really mean? No. I knew they were gigantic and cared little else about their towering height. (I'm no mountaineer and have no interest in being one. I'm glad—abstractly—that others prefer to center their lives around summiting these peaks. But, fuck, I can think of a million things I'd rather be doing.) So I went about assuming I understood what really, really high meant. I didn't think about it much.

Then one day, on a trek on the Nepali side of the Himalayas, I got a new sight angle at these towering mountains.

After a day of unexpected switchbacks and continual false summits, we reached a plateau. It was the highest altitude I had ever been. Straight in front of me were the Himalayas, unobstructed. The mountains and I seemed to look at each other face-to-face. They stretched up higher into the atmosphere than I thought possible. I felt wonderfully like a tiny ant staring at a skyscraper.

It was here, on the Annapurna Circuit Trek with Sam, that I understood I needed a lot more "really" before my definition of really, really high when thinking about the Himalayas. I needed an even bigger perspective to conceptualize them.

Like with the Cross Borneo Trek, I had been in Nepal years before, heard about the Annapurna Circuit, and brought Sam with me to do the epic trek when our schedules allowed. I chose this trek in particular within the many Nepal offers because of its relative accessibility and lack of required planning. (I was busy with too many work projects to plan a complex trip.) In the right season and with easily obtained permits, you can just show up and start walking.

The walk itself is what's called a teahouse trek. You eat and sleep at these cute teahouses along the trek, so you don't have to worry about food or shelter. You can even pay someone to carry your stuff, but that's unnecessary. On other, harder treks in Nepal, sure. This circuit trek is relatively accessible and easygoing (at least compared to other high-mountain treks).

As the name implies, the trek is a loop. You follow it 145 miles deep into the mountains, over a pass, and then back down—usually in about twenty-one days. The trek centers around the 26,550-foot Annapurna mountain (the tenth-highest mountain in the world).

We planned to walk those 145 miles because the trek is a lovely way to access beautiful wilderness in Nepal's largest protected area, the Annapurna Conservation Area. Across Nepal there are currently forty-nine protected areas, making up almost 24 percent of the country's landmass.

Of those forty-nine, the Annapurna Conservation Area is my favorite. So much of Nepal's scenery is spectacular, and the Annapurna region is the best of the best. Plus, it's a hotspot of cultural and biological diversity. The Himalayas stretch over five countries (Pakistan, India, Nepal, Bhutan, and China) and have always been a place of cultural exchange and conflict. Traders have always gone through this region. They just might be on a motorcycle or in a jeep today.

The trail circumscribes this area, passing through small villages and rhododendron forests, and topping out at Thorong

La pass, at an elevation of 17,769 feet. Almost continually from the trail, you have views of the Himalayas that seem worthy of the cover of *National Geographic*. It's easy to understand why so many of its inhabitants revere this area as sacred.

I would often stop on the trail to gaze up at them. These peaks are dramatic. Their colors are deep and varied. Depending on the sunlight, time of day, and month, they're anywhere from a light dusty blue to deep steel to hot pink-orange. The whiteness of the clouds is often stark against the gray-brown of the mountainside.

One day, while staring at the jaggedness of the peaks in contrast to the softness of the fluffy-looking clouds, I realized something was odd about the order of the two: The clouds drifted below the mountains' summits. The peaks reached up into the seeming infinite of the sky, uninhibited by the usual scale of our planet.

These mountains make the Rockies look cute, like seventh-graders who tell you they're almost in high school. Compared to that, the Himalayas were Professor Emeritus status.

I still don't really know how to conceptualize the Himalayas' size fully, but I do know that a different perspective clued me in to just how little I understood. Even now I think my brain still needs to stretch farther to fit them. I probably won't ever be able to fit these towering mountains inside my head.

I think about perspective a lot, especially visual perspective. I'm not talking only in the abstract when I talk about the different ways we see the world. It's also something I've had to deal with physically. You see, my eyes don't work like a normal person's eyes. I have several visual processing disorders—my eyes don't always coordinate well together, horizontally track along smoothly, or naturally do things like see in the peripherals. When tired, I can completely lose my ability to see. When slightly less tired, I can accidentally grab words from different lines of text, mush them together, and read a very different version from what's written on the page.

Since seventh grade, I've been to optometrists, but none had caught these vision problems before. I didn't have trouble in school—I figured out workarounds to my problems, based on the assumption that we all see like how I see. You get tired; your vision completely blurs. I figured this was normal. Apparently not.

I didn't realize this until I saw a new optometrist when I moved to Los Angeles at age twenty-nine. I came in complaining that I needed a stronger prescription for nighttime driving. The doctor looked at me for a few beats, clearly pondering something, and then asked some odd questions. Like: Is my phone clear when I look at it with my glasses on? I was aghast at this question. Why in the world would I ever look at my phone with my distance glasses on? I'd be so incredibly nauseous.

It turns out I needed vision therapy to help my eyes learn to coordinate together, which is much harder to do in low light.

Changing your perspective is hard. Vision therapy was exhausting. I started learning about terms like eye tracking and eye teaming—and that not everyone closes one eye when reading dense text or thinks it's easier to just memorize whole paragraphs of an important academic journal article than have to reread the damn thing.

Similarly, it never occurred to me to tell anyone that keeping track of the subscripts and superscripts in chemistry class made me nauseous. Or that I didn't see the cars in the lanes next to me while driving on a highway.

It's easy enough to understand that we all see colors differently—and can never really fully compare those differences. It's much harder—at least for me—to conceptualize that the basics of our visual perspectives might differ radically.

At first, a visual processing disorder diagnosis feels isolating. You see weird. You're not normal. Your perception is off. How did your eyes not learn to work like everyone else's?

Then I began to realize that, even without vision problems, we all process the world differently. Knowing how I do it—and working to make it as easy as possible through things like therapy—helps me better exist in the world.

There's interesting scientific research which indicates that how we physically see the world might determine our stress levels. If our eyes are comfortable and gently looking at a distance, we mentally relax. (No wonder so many of us hate all this computer work—it's physically stressful and so mentally demanding.) Understanding our perspectives and ways in which we conceptualize the world helps us better relax, calm down, and enjoy life. And isn't that the point of it all? Isn't that the point of being on an incredible walk, like the Annapurna Circuit Trek?

Then there's the change of perspective from one direction to another: We had planned to do the trek's loop in the typical direction of the walk, counterclockwise. We ended up walking up counterclockwise and turning around, heading down clockwise.

Our trekking plan started with a five-hour bus ride from Pokhara to the starting village of Besisahar, and then we planned on spending the next week walking the trek's path through villages like Nadi Bazar, Jagat, Chame, and Upper Pisang. By Day 8, we'd spend a few days acclimatizing at Manang before tackling the high pass of Thorong La on Day 11. Then we'd slowly descend through the Kali Gandaki Valley, taking about seven to ten days to reach Nayapul before jumping on a bus back to Kathmandu.

The actual trip didn't go according to plan. Sam got really sick in Pokhara. Like, *do you need to go to the hospital?* food poisoning sick. Sam is a loud vomiter, and this sickness produced the most deafening and prolific amount of vomiting I'd seen from him in the fifteen years I've known him. (You know it's a sign of true love when you can recognize your partner's vomiting.) Sam vomited so much that the two nice men who ran the tiny hotel we were staying in came to check on him and to ensure we had all the food, clean water, and ibuprofen he might need.

We didn't catch the bus to Besisahar that day. By the time we eventually made it to the trek's start, Sam still felt pretty weak. I took all the weight of our gear in my backpack. Our trek started with a plodding stumble, not a sprightly jaunt.

By the time we got to Manang, it was clear our trek was over. Altitude and the continuing effects of food poisoning had Sam feeling awful for much of our walk. It only got worse as we climbed higher into the sky. We both knew that a poorly timed stumble caused by feeling lightheaded from altitude sickness or the repercussions of food poisoning could have a catastrophic result on these cliff-lined trails.

Turning around on an adventure is never very glamorous. As the author David Grann writes about a famous turn-arounder adventurer: "Ernest Shackleton was, in many ways, a failure."

Shackleton never had an Antarctic trip go according to plan—often because he put the well-being and safety of his crew above the glory of an expeditionary first. As he said to his wife, Emily: "A live donkey is better than a dead lion, isn't it?" (She agreed.)

The decision to turn around and head back down the mountain was easy: We both agreed that a live donkey was a better existence.

I didn't think I'd love walking back down the mountain. We obviously needed to do it. Safety and health come first. That didn't mean I was exactly thrilled about hiking back through paths we had already covered instead of venturing forward into landscapes we hadn't yet seen.

I was so wrong: Hiking the same path in reverse was spectacular. The change of perspective let me notice things I somehow missed in the opposite direction. Everything felt familiar and yet also new. The fresh unfamiliarity is why if you're hiking off-trail in the backcountry, you always leave yourself clues—snapped branches, piles of rocks—of where you come from. Going in reverse creates a wildly new perspective.

Plus, walking down a mountain is so much easier than walking up. It's easier to enjoy a spectacular grove of perfuming pines when you're putting in minimal exertion passing through them.

One of the weirdest perspective-altering things we saw on our pleasant meander down the mountain was a helicopter flying in a valley below us.

I knew we were high up (Sam was feeling sick from the altitude for a reason) but had forgotten how close to the sky we had gotten. Here I was standing on flat ground, on a dirt path—not clinging to the side of a cliff or anything close to mountaineering—and yet I was looking down on a helicopter flying.

Likely it was a helicopter doing a sightseeing tour from Pokhara or bringing tourists who are low on time and willing to spend a sizable chunk of money to skip the first few days of the trek. This was not a helicopter doing a low-elevation rescue or flying in an unusual pattern. It was flying in the sky, like a typical helicopter. I was standing, looking down on it.

Just like when I was hiking in Borneo, a line from George Eliot's *Middlemarch* popped into my brain: "It is a narrow mind which cannot look at a subject from various points of view." Eliot knew about many things—and she certainly understood perspective.

I'm pretty sure Junko Tabei understood this as well. She was a supreme badass: the first woman to submit Mount Everest (thirty-sixth person overall to do so), the first woman to climb the Seven Summits (the highest peaks on each continent), and a participant in forty-four all-woman mountaineering expeditions. All this while also being a mother in 1970s Japan, largely self-fundraising for her expeditions, and working as a hiking guide and teacher.

Junko loved the summit but also found beauty in the trail itself. Describing the first time she summited a mountain as a kid, she wrote: "I loved every element. All around us, sulphur-stained holes in the ground sizzled where natural onsen came to life at our feet. I admired the juxtaposition of the heat from the springs and the cold temperatures (despite it being summer) on the mountain. The impact this had on me, the effect on my body and skin, was unforgettable. It triggered an awareness that there were many things in the world for me to discover. When we reached the summit that day, I felt a joy of achievement that I had never experienced before."

Seeing things in a new light, a new perspective—I think we've all experienced this before. When something that you think you know really well—even something as foundational as how one's body feels on this earth as a little kid—can be changed by a hike or a walk somewhere. Something shifts and all of a sudden you're seeing life in a new light. It changes us, and it changes how we view things around us.

We do this with trails and vistas—but also with other humans. How often do we think we know everything there is to know about a person, only to have them say something (profound, dumb, out of the blue, or about a topic we didn't know they knew deeply) and have it radically change how we see them?

Standing there on the trail in Nepal, I felt like you do when you look out an airplane window and see tiny houses below you. Before you see the miniature things on the ground, it's easy to pretend that you're not speeding through the sky. The clouds don't quickly move past your window nor are they that big. You notice their puffs and fluffs and curves, not what their dimensions must be for the physics equation to work: If I'm moving at 450 to 575 mph through a cloud for 45 seconds, how large must this cloud be? How large must all those other clouds be? Can my brain even hold those sizes?

How am I hiking at an easy exertion and looking down on a helicopter flying? This is what I mean when I say good nonsense. This trek isn't silly, but it's not unimportant. It's something one does for awe, flow, curiosity, and adventure. It allows you a whole different perspective.

Seeing a helicopter from above emphasized that things are not always what they seem. I also felt lucky to be prioritizing the silliness of a walk, of prioritizing that a journey should be enjoyable and safe, not done for abstract achievements—rather than taking a helicopter to only trek the high-altitude pass of the circuit, skipping almost all of what Sam and I would actually cover on this trip.

People talk about Type II fun—that type where it's only fun in retrospect but not in the moment. For many, recreation seems to be about how hard they suffered. The Annapurna Circuit Trek wasn't a sufferfest but an example of rejuvenation, stress, hard effort, recreation, leisure, and pleasure. It was also a practice in understanding limits and turning around. Some moments were challenging—they weren't the entire thing. I think that's the critical bit: Almost the whole trek was enjoyable.

Even playful at times. One afternoon we got false-charged by a sizable yak with large horns. It was my fault. Like a sane person, I assumed yaks don't understand English (or any other spoken human language). I looked at the yak and said to Sam, "That coat would make an amazing sweater." The yak looked up and started running at us with impressive speed, in a manner that seemed, to me at least, to convey that it was not yet done with its wool, please and thank you.

To my credit, it would make a beautiful knitted item. The yak's fur was a nice, rich brown-yellow-orange. The wool from yaks is naturally shed in the spring and is warmer and softer than any other type of wool.

The yak stopped short of actually hitting us. (It being the one completely in control of the situation, not us.) And, to be clear, I understand it was likely just me talking aloud that alerted (and perhaps scared) the yak to our presence—not the fact that I was eyeing it for my next sweater.

I don't think adventure has to be a sufferfest or achieve anything. I didn't always feel this way, but I'm glad I do now. It's something being around Sam taught me. He's one of those kind souls who somehow has always understood that it's essential to enjoy things and not cram yourself through discomfort.

Our storytelling of adventures sometimes forgets this. It can swing too far into the territory that valorizes suffering, self-harm, pain caves, and pushing through problems instead of thoughtfully fixing them. Too often in recounting our adventures we seem to have an urge to remind the listener that the experience was justifiable because *I didn't have chill fun, I had painful fun so it's okay that I did it.*

Adventure has moments of unpleasantness, for sure. But that's not the only thing to it. Why then is this how we tell our stories?

Perhaps it is because an adventure is so expansive that it becomes hard to convey to another person. It's like Proust's petite madeleine cakes. To focus on the discrete phenomena is to pull at the experience of everything.

I always wonder: Does attempting to describe a phenomenon narrow the experience of it? I suppose it's a question without a genuine answer—kinda like the joke that most *New Yorker* articles subheading questions will be answered in the article's text with "yes . . . and no."

I guess also I'm talking about the mistake of assuming adventure requires supreme examples of action and chaos. You can just be on an adventure. You don't have to *do*. So much of adventure storytelling is through action verbs rather than descriptive language. How you choose to describe your experience and what rhetoric you use matter.

That's what Christiane Ritter, the Austrian painter who wrote about spending a year in the Arctic in 1933 in her book *A Woman in the Polar Night*, and even Proust seem to understand.

Ritter leaves out utilitarian facts of her daily life, the less esoteric information. We don't know: How and where did she go to the bathroom in this frozen world? Did she ever cry out of frustration at her situation?

Ritter gives us a rare glimpse into what adventure storytelling could be outside of the sufferfest rhetoric. The British travel writer Sara Wheeler, who has extensive adventure experience in both the Arctic and Antarctica, contributed a foreword to *A Woman in the Polar Night*. In it she wrote, "Women's voices are seldom heard in the polar regions. Unlike most male accounts this one is not about breaking records or beating the Arctic into submission like a mammoths outside a cave."

Sometimes our adventure tales today swing too far into selecting the utilitarian over the aesthetic. Hardship and gore provide drama that drives stories of adventure survival. Dampen the dramatic language a bit, and you'll usually find a story premised on ego-driven unnecessary risks and a lack of foresight leading to insufficient food supplies. Boring. Give me Ritter's colors over that garbage.

Jane Robinson, a British historian who focuses on women's stories that too often go untold, collected the travel writings of historical (mostly rich and white) British women in her book *Wayward Women*. Having read so much travel writing from a time when the genders were so widely separated into an unequal binary, she discovered an interesting division: Women's travel writing covered the how and the why. Men's focused on the what and the where.

In a culture where women rarely traveled, their reiteration of the travels needed (or seemed to need) to answer the confused audience's questions. They wanted to know of the women travelers: How did you do this? Why do this?

Men, the more expected traveling gender, didn't explain. They report: I did this activity there.

We (luckily) don't split our writing so neatly along a gendered binary anymore, but the How/Why and What/Where divide remains. When you need more drama, more nuance in a trip report that explains only the What and Where, authors too often reach for suffering and hardship to supplement the narrative. But in doing so, we communicate it is the sufferfest aspect that makes for an adventure. It is a narrative that forgets that not being in pain, actually enjoying your recreation, is just as valuable as a hard or painful recreation. A painful experience isn't necessarily better.

Losing perspective on our priorities in life can have deadly consequences in the wilderness. (People die all the time on the Annapurna Circuit Trek—not because the trek itself is deadly strenuous, but because they forget to prioritize health and safety.) To quote Sara Wheeler again: "As far as I was then aware, the continent [Antarctica] was little more than a testing ground for men with frozen beards to see how dead they could get."

That's not my idea of a good time.

About a week into the trek (before we turned around), we hit what seemed like an entire mountainside of switchbacks and false summits. It was humbling in the best way. Herds of goats passed us, their bells ringing out into the vastness of the valley below us. I wanted to rush up to the top but literally could not. Instead, I had to resign myself to whatever slow pace the altitude and steep incline forced upon us. My attention would sometimes zoom into every step but more often it took a wider lens. There was just too much to see and hear not to try and take it all in.

At every switchback, it felt like we couldn't possibly be expected to still walk higher up into the atmosphere—that it shouldn't be physically possible to be walking at this altitude. Yet we did. We trudged along at dizzyingly high heights with spectacular views of the tallest peaks in the distance. We were already so high in the sky (and climbing higher by the slowly passing minute), and those peaks still looked to be the same impossibly high heights. Compared to the scale of the Himalayas, our days of hiking and arduous switchbacks hadn't changed much about our elevation.

The trail continued upwards, often filled with other hikers and residents of the region. People living in the Annapurna Conservation Area are mostly of Gurung and Magar ethnicity. They're largely herders and farmers—and increasingly, working in the tourism business. As we passed, they sometimes shouted out greetings to us. Mostly, they focused on their potato digging, their laundry, and their lives.

Bells jingling meant horses or goats (and their accompanying humans) likely wanted to pass by us—or a yak in a nearby field was on the move. An engine's roar meant jump to the side of the road quickly, a jeep or motorcycle is hauling itself up these tight paths. I saw motorcycles on paths I was nervous to walk on, where the side dropped off thousands of feet and the path was narrow, littered with loose rocks and twisting around blind curves.

Different types of walking create distinct thoughts. Borneo's path is narrow and easily missed; I think myopically and in the eternal present. Copenhagen's streets provide a safe wandering. The Annapurna Circuit's (mostly) wide trails, slow pace, and human noises create broad thoughts that combine the otherworldly and deeply human.

Nepal offers plenty of stunning vistas to shake off your feelings of mundane existence and provides a sometimes overwhelming amount of stairs to be slowly tackled. It's a wonderful coupling, best seen and thought about through the movements of a trek—astonishment taken one plodding step after the next.

Playing from a perspective of astonishment makes it easier to remember the larger context of our lives, to inhabit good nonsense. We're tiny little things on a tiny planet in a remote corner of the universe. Even in the scale of life on Earth, we're just a blip in that story. Hell, even in the story of humans on Earth, we're a footnote.

I like being reminded it all doesn't matter. It lets me focus on what really counts: love, joy, play, kindness. It's why I studied anthropology in college. The precise peculiarity of how we choose to live our daily lives is up to us—and isn't a given.

The utter diversity of ways humans have lived (and some still do) still surprises me. History, archaeology, and cultural anthropology remind us it hasn't always been like this and doesn't have to be like this. They provide proof of extremely different ways of interpreting daily life. We collectively and individually have made choices to live our lives like this, for better or worse.

How we tell stories about our past—why and what aspects we include and what we decide to bracket out—is fascinating. As any good archaeologist will say to you, those stories are sometimes much more revealing about present-day politics than about the history the story is purporting to tell. Some places I've worked as an archaeologist do just that—they get used to tell stories about the past but then, in turn, are used to tell us important things about the future.

Societies collapsed because of political instability, war, famine, climatic changes. People continued on, creating new ways of being.

The past often gets used to warn us about impending doom. There are also the narratives of people loving one another, hanging out with friends, making art, and goofing around. It's just a bit harder to find concrete evidence of those things in the historical and archaeological record.

These are the types of sweaty concepts I think about on a trip. I talked about this in the book's introduction. Sweaty concepts are great to play with when you're out doing something physical.

Sweaty concepts are bodily. We feel them in our body. Our body is something often left out of accounts of adventure and in history (unless it's a gruesome, gory detail like toes removed because of frostbite or French Revolution beheadings). As an anthropologist, I study things that are physical. Our lives are physical, even when we're in supposedly virtual worlds. Out here on this hike is physical.

Here's an example: when and how to go to the bathroom.

Attending to bathroom needs in the wilderness is one of the first things you teach a new hiker. Sometimes it involves a freshly dug hole. Sometimes, like on the Annapurna Circuit Trek, it involves real toilets in cute teahouses.

Bare with me here—because toilets are actually hugely important to how we study societies. Toilets are (usually) mundane to us today. And yet, poop illuminates so much more about our past than do the great architectural works we visit as a tourist. Coprolites, ancient feces, are some of the most amazing portals to past societies, even the prehistoric one. A single piece reveals diet, habitat, health, and so much more. It is a much more dynamic piece of evidence than a building, cathedral, or pyramid. Where that poop shows up—ancient or more recent—is also quite telling.

Flush toilets and indoor plumbing pop up (and disappear) in the archaeological and historical records worldwide in many eras—and often independent of one another. It makes sense: Sanitarily dealing with our waste is of supreme importance to the health of a society—and there are many ways to do it. There are many government officials focused on—and creating policy around—how to properly deal with the vast amount of human waste created by all the tourists walking the Annapurna Circuit.

How we talk about that waste is also revealing. Have you noticed almost all of our swear words are bodily words? They focus on human acts and waste—the corporeal seemingly so disgusting we've turned the muckiest of it into swear words. It makes sense: Words we use for our most extreme feelings use that physicality.

I think it's kinda fucking amazing.

Profanities decorate my thoughts and adventures (as they do for most of us). Swear words provide delightful verbal punctuation. They instantly communicate everything from *I think we're in trouble* to *Wow, this vista is beautiful.*

Realize that Sam is quite sick and needs not to be doing this trek? *Fuck. Fuck. Fuck.* Find out that the teahouses on the Annapurna Circuit only serve weak Nescafé coffee? *Oh shiiiit.* Think about the elevation gain you're about to trek up? *That's gonna fucking hurt.* Someone who thinks women can't adventure? *Dumbass.*

Swear words are linguistic shape-shifting miracles akin only to the word *like* in their ability to masterfully perform as different parts of a sentence. They easily spill out of an adventurer's mouth (and a New Yorker's).

My favorite way to utilize them is to express delight at the feeling of awe. One such moment occurred at night on the trail in Nepal, when I couldn't sleep much because I was worried about Sam being sick. I went for a walk and looked up.

I saw the Milky Way on a cloudless, moonless night far removed from light pollution. I could try to do descriptive justice here to what I saw and maybe even find some research to give scientific context of the galactic wonder. Really, though, the best way to sum it up is: *holy shit.*

It's the best way I know how to accurately, succinctly convey the beauty I saw and the wonder I felt. I feel that way anytime I see stars—*astonished.*

Part II

FLOAT

Chapter 4

Playing in Raja Ampat

You don't swim when you dive; you fly.

An easy way to spot a new diver: They're trying to swim. To navigate themself underwater, they're ignoring physics and moving about as if they were on the water's surface, at a lap pool. They kick and flail, and don't glide by using their breath and slowly moving each leg and hip.

A new diver kicks hard. They don't know how to slow themself down, to move through this new medium of physical space. Water is a liquid, not a gas. A novice diver thrashes about, tiring themself out quickly, consuming their air tank with rapid speed.

Diving requires a slow, consistent float, and it isn't much physical exertion. These movements create a forced meditation. You have to focus on the immediate now, which just happens to be filled with some of the most amazing, weird-looking creatures.

Thoughts come with ease and tend to be gentle. They're slow to appear and slow to leave. My attention meanders from thought to thought as my visual field softly but consistently changes. As I float physically, it's easy to float mentally into a state of otherworldliness that mimics the alternate, underwater reality I'm looking at.

To dive you must use your whole body to fly underwater while also giving in to the larger forces around you. Play within those forces rather than fight against them.

A basic understanding of physics controls your speed. Slow down: Place your body closer to a nearby physical object, like a wall or the ocean floor. Speed up: Move away from nearby objects, inching out into the open blue ocean.

Diving movements are mainly in reaction to the surrounding objects. There's often something physical to tie yourself into the landscape, to relax into your surroundings. It could be a rock wall filled with coral and nudibranchs, a seabed floor near where a giant school of barracuda swirl, beds of coral with colorful fish, caves where sharks like to hide out, or underwater mountain peaks where mantas like to have their skin cleaned by tiny fish.

Most of what you're doing is floating as you breathe, with the aid of a tank below the surface, consuming the oxygen mixture with patient sips to make it last as long as possible. That way, you can see as many odd and beautiful creatures as your tank's volume allows. The less you flail, the less oxygen you need to consume. The more you float, the more leisure you get.

Navigating your floating body requires inhales, exhales, and horizontal leans. I promise: It's just physics. You're an object in a body of water. Want to float higher? Make your inhales longer than your exhales. Lower? Do the opposite. Go somewhere specific? Lean towards where you want to go. (In diving and life.) The current and your slowly pumping legs will bring you there.

I learned how to scuba dive on a whim in 2011. After quitting an awful job doing agricultural research, I found myself in Asia with time to kill. I had friends in Thailand and so went there. People had told me over the years that I might like scuba diving and now seemed like the right time (and place). After a few fun weeks in Thailand's north with my friends, I wanted to go try scuba diving and so headed south to the country's islands.

There, on the tiny island of Koh Phi Phi, I learned to scuba dive. I stayed in a little hut close to the ocean and filled with cute geckos, a terrible bed, and a slow ceiling fan. It was perfection. I spent two weeks there, walking each morning from my hut, through the jungle and along the ocean, to the dive shop. Because it was almost off-season, I was the only student in my diving courses.

I settled into a calm, easygoing state of mind. It's the perspective this type of travel seems to easily bring about—when you're on a small island, alone, and there just to learn something.

Something just clicked on my first dive: It was easy. It was thrilling. It was beautiful. And, perhaps most wonderfully, it was freeing. It felt like I'd been doing it my whole life.

We only floated a few feet below the surface, but that was deep enough to feel like I had entered another reality. It was a world in which parrotfish swam past my face, blacktip reef sharks meandered below me, and moray eels side-eyed me. Soft coral waved with the gentle currents and hard corals stood resolute—bright and oddly shaped, as if from an alien planet.

In retrospect, compared to other dives I've since been on, I didn't actually see that much. That's good—you don't want beginner divers, who are unable to control their movements, banging into fragile coral or venomous lionfish. I didn't know on my first dive that what I was seeing was a mostly sandy spot with commonplace creatures. All I understood was that *holy shit that's a fish* and *look at me float like it's floating!*

The water in Thailand, especially at shallow depths, is warm. The currents, especially close to shore and where beginner divers are taken, are gentle. The combination feels like the best bathtub. Even with all the dive equipment on my body, I quickly forgot where my body ended and where the ocean began.

My instructor, a stern British man, made sure I knew the safety protocols inside out. After two weeks with him I could comfortably (and safely) finish a dive, even if my mask came off. I knew what it felt like to start to have my nitrogen levels rise too high, making me act drunk, and could get myself to safety. One of the most important lessons was that sinking too deep or changing depths (up and down) too quickly can kill you. Shooting up to the surface too fast can give you the bends—a cutely named, potentially deadly situation where nitrogen forms bubbles in your tissue and bloodstream. He made sure I could (and still can) rescue myself and others in a multitude of situations.

In the days and years that followed that meander to southern Thailand, I've visited many magical underwater spots in Southeast Asia and Australia. I prefer going where strong currents flow, reefs are full of vibrant life, and the above-water landscape is full of tropical islands.

Some of the most fantastic diving can be found in what's known as the Coral Triangle. It's a marine area with a triangle-ish shape encompassing parts of Papua New Guinea, Timor-Leste, Solomon Islands, Malaysia, the Philippines, and Indonesia. Within that triangle lives some of the most biodiversity found in any marine environment in the world.

The middle of the Coral Triangle—and the best part— is Raja Ampat. Located in the eastern corner of Indonesia, Raja Ampat is remote even by Indonesian standards. Getting there from Jakarta, the country's capital, takes multiple flights with long layovers. It once took me twenty-four hours to get from Jakarta to Sorong, the nearest airport to dive sites in Raja Ampat.

Sorong isn't where the best diving is. Like most of Indonesia, Sorong has dive sites right off its shores, but even better dive sites are further out. So once you've gotten to Sorong, you still need to get on a boat—or a ferry to a boat— for many hours before you're jumping into the water with your dive gear.

I mostly dive off of liveaboards—it's much cheaper per dive and easier to get to remote dive spots. If you're sleeping on the boat, there's no rush to hurry back to shore after a dive. Instead of a quick turnaround and rush to pack your gear, you can lie on the boat's deck and warm up. The mix of sun and humidity warms you up as the sea breeze slightly cools you down. I love coming back to the boat after a dive.

As you sit on the deck, you talk with all the other humans on the boat about your collective shared solitary experiences underwater. What fish did you see? How cool was that shark? Are you cold still?

Much of Raja Ampat is within a well-monitored conservation area. Given its tremendous biological diversity, a lot of money and political attention have gone into restoring and protecting the region, especially in the last decade. Only around forty liveaboards are allowed within the very large conservation area at a given time—and they usually coordinate so that each is the only boat at a given dive site. It's pretty common to not see another liveaboard at all—and to only see the infrequent small boat transferring locals around the region or fishermen catching dinner.

Raja Ampat's dive spots are usually on the deeper side—around thirty to a hundred feet. Down there, you'll find everything from the hot pink, spotted, one-inch pygmy seahorse to an abundance of large sharks to schools of fish that swirl about you. There's so much to look at.

On our second-to-last dive of my liveaboard trip there in 2017, I was delightedly looking at a literal rainbow's worth of colors in the coral growing on an underwater pinnacle. Out of the corner of my eye, I saw a dark, giant shape swoop by me. Then another. And another. I looked up and saw ten creatures, each the size of a school bus. Oceanic mantas had arrived.

Oceanic mantas reach thirty feet across their wingspan, tip-to-tip, and weigh up to 6,600 pounds. They're almost triangle-shaped, with their tips and tail making the three points. Their faces are shaped by two giant prongs protruding out of either side of a large mouth. Technically those prongs are called cephalic fins, but they look like horns that can move and frame their mouths.

I'm pretty sure I could easily fit inside a manta's mouth. (I haven't tried.) That large mouth isn't for biting humans— mantas have no teeth—but rather for scooping up and swallowing tiny plankton and fish. Mantas use their cephalic fins to funnel in dinner. They also probably use these prongs to communicate with one another.

So, oddly shaped buses, but bus-sized nonetheless. These giants showed up, hurtling at us out of seemingly nowhere, and wanted to play.

Those ten oceanic mantas played with us for the hour that our scuba tanks allowed us in the below-water world. They swooped, glided, and dived at us.

One reason mantas will come close to calm divers is that they like to play with your out-gassed air bubbles when you scuba dive. They let the bubbles tickle their bellies. Maybe there's a more practical reason for the behavior. Perhaps it helps clean their delicate skin in the same symbiotic way remora fish can do for mantas. But it sure feels like play— like how a big, friendly dog plays with you. Why can't it be both?

For an hour, the mantas did loops: a quick bubble belly tickle followed by a zoom up to the surface, where the manta would shoot out of the water, belly flop, and come swooping back down to us. It was like being surrounded by giddy puppies looking to show off and zooming around with excitement.

Playing with mantas always makes me think about what Montaigne wrote about his cat: "When I play with my cat, who knows if I am not a pastime to her more than she is to me?"

Montaigne, the French sixteenth-century writer who saw his best friend die of the black plague and his country continue its brutal religious civil wars, spent many of his days in his library, reading and writing—and playing with his cat. By seeing himself through the eyes of his cat, and other such moments of recognizing aliveness, Montaigne created his entire philosophy of what it means to live.

Like other mantas I've dived near, the mantas in Raja Ampat inspected us as we inspected them. Excited ones did the joyous belly-flop laps. Calmer ones showed their spotted bellies and large gill slits as they glided around us. (Each manta's belly spots are specific to the individual, like our fingerprints.) They all look at you through eyes that look startlingly like enlarged human eyes. The intelligence and curiosity ooze off these creatures. You feel their aliveness when you meet them, diving underwater.

Being in the underwater magic of the world helps me be playful. I always come back to Patricia Hampl's book, *The Art of the Wasted Day*, and her point that life is floating and some of the best parts of that floating are "effortless and aware."

It's only by inhabiting such a state that you can notice that a manta might be playing with you.

Science backs up the feelings of intelligence you get when diving with them. Mantas pass the self-recognition mirror test—they understand they're looking at themselves and not meeting another creature. Dogs and cats don't pass the test. Elephants do pass. We humans pass this test but only after the age of two or so.

It is an incredibly imprecise way of measuring intelligence—a creature's conscious understanding of self needs to outwardly mimic our own movements of recognizing ourselves in a mirror. The test likely fails to acknowledge many an intelligent animal. And yet, it clearly shows that mantas are not only smart but also conscious of themselves in the same physicality as are we.

Mantas look radically different from us, but it turns out we do the same *ooh how's my nose looking today?* movements in front of a mirror when given a chance.

I couldn't believe how cool it was to play with mantas. They can dive deeper into the ocean than our technology can track. Mantas are so mysterious that we don't know many basic facts about them that we often take for granted for other large species: details about how they raise their young, specifics about their diets, what they do down in the dark depths of the ocean where we can't go. By tracking photos, often ones taken by vacationing scuba divers, scientists can figure out where individual mantas (known by their fingerprint-like belly spots) travel. We've realized that ocean mantas travel almost the entire oceanic world, visiting the warm, tropical waters of Raja Ampat and subtropical waters but also the chillier temperate waters of Mexico and Japan.

Similar to the gentle giants on land that are mountain gorillas, oceanic mantas reach sexual maturity relatively late in their lifespan and only have one pup at a time. (Mountain gorillas also pass the mirror test.) For both endangered species, this creates a population math problem. Habitat destruction and poaching destroy their numbers faster than the population can reproduce.

Oceanic mantas are endangered—we don't know how many remain, but we do know that their numbers are likely decreasing. It can be emotionally hard to watch mantas play while knowing how quickly their numbers are dwindling, wondering if I'll still be able to dive with them in fifty years.

What do you do with the wonder and awe you feel when ten bus-sized giants of the ocean have come to play with you?

It's a call to pause and rest in the moment. But, of course, that's hard to do when currents are flopping you about. It's hard to do in life in general. We want to savor moments when we sense the world's awe. Too easily, at least for me, my attention can wander away—sometimes, paradoxically, to thinking about how to get more moments of wonder in my life, forgetting to appreciate the magic in front of me.

A pause is an intentional relaxation, an intentional rest. It's harder to do in water than on land. To relax underwater is a conscious relaxation. You could drown, after all.

Relaxation is a more comfortable way of living, but it's also a key to surviving tricky situations underwater. If you're being thrown about by strong currents or, say, surprised by a curious pair of thresher sharks in a cave, you have to get meditative about it: Your intention must be to bring your intention to the moment. Stiff, jerky movements will not help here. Nor will a panicking mind.

When you're underwater with a tank, you have to make sure you don't panic. It's also something that trains us to not panic when we're back on shore—and say, cut off in traffic.

Once I do relax into my watery surroundings, I find that my brain relaxes differently on land than it does below water. Air is much less dense than water. It creates much less resistance. Because you have to pay more attention underwater, the quality of the relaxation you can get into is more expansive than on land.

Underwater I can more easily forget where I stop and where the rest of the world begins. I think it's something to do with the water. Moving through water changes how my brain interacts with its surroundings. I enter a more expansive thinking.

I float. I stretch out. My limbs relax, and my thoughts follow.

Underwater it's slightly easier to physically (and thus mentally) enact a pause. When the ten mantas appeared, each diver did what you do when some cool creatures show up: keep yourself in one place and watch.

The easiest way to do that requires only two fingers. With your pointer and thumb, you pinch the nearest rock (checking first it isn't coral or another creature). You hold your spot as the strong current tries to throw you up, down, or sideways. That pinch steadies you in one place, letting you be as distracted by the wildlife as possible.

Distracted, you see a rainbow of colors in the corals. Mantas might come to play with your off-gassed bubbles. If you're smart, you'll know to pause in the chaos of the current.

There are safe and unsafe ways to let yourself get distracted underwater. The safe way—a pinch of a rock—lets you get enough, but not completely, distracted. Complete distraction while diving can kill.

You can accidentally drift far away or forget to check the level of air in your tank. A lack of breathable air underwater spells bad news. As does floating out to sea, lost and unable to be rescued.

Almost all my favorite dive spots are too far from the nearest hospital to save your life if you change depths too fast and get the bends. Knowing a dive spot well or going with someone who does can also mean life or death. Currents change at different times of the day, even in the same location. A deadly, downward-spiraling whirlpool might be there at 11 a.m. but not at 2 p.m. Timing matters.

Our bodies can handle a surprising amount of things underwater—and special equipment helps. Yet those bodies aren't infallible, especially underwater. Without paying attention, it's easy to forget where your body is in space and how long you've been down there. Space and time get murky underwater. Above water, too.

You can't exactly miss a manta the size of a bus. But to spot some of the other magical creatures, you really do need to pay attention to detail to notice them. When you do, these worlds open up that are as magnificent as the mantas. That noticing invites delight, which leads to play.

In the mid-1990s, kayaking guide and writer Jennifer Hahn solo kayaked 750 miles along the Inside Passage from Alaska to Washington State in three distinct parts over springs and summers. She kayaked those hundreds of miles along the coasts of Alaska, British Columbia, and the Pacific Northwest for the sake of doing it—and noticing what she noticed along the way.

Hahn fills her book, *Spirited Waters*, with recipes to make from wild food and details of her foraged dinners. At one point she spent two days and nights resting on an islet near Milbanke Sound. There she spent much of her time watching a family of otters play, relax, eat, and protect the young pups from a hungry eagle. The two pups play tug-of-war with each other and try to help the mother otter dig for snails to eat. Hahn, too, eats snails. Hers are limpet snails taken off low-tide rocks. The otters eat moon snails from the muddy shores. Her ability to forage adds a depth to her noticing. While I might notice a snail, Hahn sees two different species of snails for two wildly different dinners.

I've kayaked a small fraction of the route Hahn covered: the British Columbian route from Bella Bella to Port Hardy over three weeks. There's much to notice there: Orcas surface, easily outpacing you. Steller sea lions play uncomfortably close to your easily flipped kayak. Bald eagles become as commonplace as pigeons in New York City. When the sun pokes through the clouds, it streams onto a thick, dark, lush temperate rainforest from which pockets of fog rise, heated by the unexpected solar rays.

Underwater the most common sea star is the *Pisaster ochraceus*, a thick, knobby creature ranging in color from bright yellow to deep purple. It eats mussels and barnacles, both of which—along with the sea stars and other creatures— can easily be seen in shallow waters near shores. But, it's only one of many types of sea stars living in British Columbia.

There are so many types in this biodiversity hotspot that scientists are still literally counting the number of species of sea stars—as well as many other creatures.

Near the end of her long kayaking journey, Hahn asks: "What have we lost by not listening? I wondered. Out there, with no human companions, my heart longed to speak with some thing. Before I left on my solo journey, people often asked, 'Won't you get lonely? How can you handle so much solitude?' Now I knew the answer.

It is this: We must talk with many things. Seals and eagles. Water and wind. Columbine flowers and spruce trees. Land snails and lichens. By broadening our idea of companions, we discover we don't so much experience solitude, as multitude."

I get it. When I'm out there, alone, it doesn't feel solitary. The excited electrons in everything become tangible. Nonhuman creatures become sentient with agency and personality. They had it the whole time, of course. Without listening, without paying attention, their companionship is easy to miss.

Sometimes it takes some solitude to find that multitude. Solitude, away from human companions, can be our best method of becoming ourselves and thus recognizing our part in the world—and the other creatures that inhabit it.

In some ways, I've never felt more of that mix of solitude and multitude in the wilderness than when kayaking—even with others around. In the hush of synchronized movement over days and weeks with those with whom you're very familiar, you can forget the presence of other humans. It's the same sort of feeling of being alone even as others dive nearby. You keep an eye on the others but have large stretches without needed communication. You're alone, together.

Letting multitude exist in our lives is more fun. You get to see how other creatures play—and maybe even use you for their play. It helps move us out of the constant spotlight our egos wish to put on us and centers other creatures, other things, in the world alongside us.

Whales are creatures we know sing, play, and exist in worlds beyond us, alongside us. More than once, they appear next to Hahn's kayak, sometimes surfacing quite close to her. Such closeness allows her to know the companionship these creatures provide and extrapolate that to the entire universe.

Multitude lets us consider the plethora of life—sentient life—around us. That richness always makes me feel smaller, in a nice way, and reminds me to take life less seriously.

Sara Wheeler, the travel writer who, as I mentioned in Chapter 3, understands adventure stories don't require hyper-masculine sufferfest rhetoric, has a lovely quote in her book *Terra Incognita* about the companionship of the other: "'Were you ever lonely?' asked Tony. 'Once. At the beginning of the last week I awoke one night in a tent and thought, 'What is wrong? I feel like I am in a dream.' Then I realized the wind had dropped. I had been in this wind for six weeks, and you know, it had been a companion.'" Multitude doesn't need to be another species. It can be a meteorological phenomenon.

We rarely think about the wind as a companion because it is silent. Like so much else in our world, it can fade into the background, unnoticed, until we have the space away from other humans to feel the multitude. Or, when it makes itself so noisily a presence that we can't ignore it.

The wind speaks through others. That quiet can make it easily ignored. What would it mean to listen to the wind, not just when it howls and shakes the trees? What would it mean to listen to our nonhuman companions on this planet? How do we find that multitude, not rarely, but often?

The reefs in Raja Ampat are relatively healthy—they can support millions of tiny crustaceans as well as the giant mantas playing with us. Other places aren't so lucky—they're dying. We lost about 14 percent of our global ocean's reefs in the last decade alone. Likely, Raja Ampat someday soon won't be so lucky either. Warming waters, acidification, and pollution are happening here too. If I think about this death while I'm diving, all of a sudden I'm not playing anymore. I'm instead mourning what is yet to have died.

It's amazing how quickly our thoughts can flip. Even here in paradise. Even here swimming with these creatures. Our minds can see the underside of everything we notice. How much fuel does the liveaboard use? Is it even that much when compared to the airplanes I took to get to Indonesia? What about my wetsuit? Its neoprene is a petroleum-derived product. Fossil-free ones are often made from limestone, which has its own problems. Even the super expensive, more environmentally friendly ones are made from natural rubber. That rubber is harvested from trees grown on plantations, which are too frequently created from bulldozing down tropical rainforests.

Indonesia is the second-largest producer of natural rubber in the world. Being above water and between dives doesn't let me escape these sweaty concepts. Jungled islands surround all of my favorite dive spots in Indonesia. In those jungles, creatures chatter and screech. Gold-mining river machines and chain saws also roar. Not always, not everywhere, but too often.

You can't hear the gold mining or deforestation while diving, as you sometimes can while hiking. But it's never very far from my thoughts. I see the wood of the boat we're sleeping on at night and wonder where it came from. Was it sourced correctly? What does it even mean to correctly source killing another living thing?

I see the flash of my gold jewelry and wonder about where it came from and what (not if) types of destruction occurred to put this shiny, pretty metal in my hand.

Gold can be found in the rivers of Indonesia, particularly Borneo. On land as well. Mining for that gold today takes many shapes. Some are industrial, large deep pits that seemingly go into the middle of the earth. Others are mining boats whose engines scream as they suck up the river water, stilt, and perhaps gold through a filter. Still others are an old Dayak couple with a portable diesel engine, a hose, and a woven shallow basket. Theirs is the same concept as the river boats—just much slower (and somewhat quieter).

I don't mean to pick on gold and wood. Pull at anything we consume: There's likely an ugly underbelly of truth. It hurts to remember these truths and somehow keep playing.

The movements of playful floating help me meander through the paradox of holding feelings of joy and sadness at the same time—of holding life with the touch of good nonsense. When in water there somehow seems to be enough space in my brain for both to exist (sometimes).

It's useful to be able to feel that paradox, even if I don't fully understand it. We come from a culture that knows too much about hurt—and how to push it away. We can't tolerate any discomfort in our feelings. So we bury ourselves in the grind, in fitness, in work, in mindless distraction.

It's much harder to muscle through water than air. It becomes incredibly obvious if you're flapping about, wasting precious oxygen and probably not letting yourself have an easy time. We need to let ourselves feel the currents, feel the hurt, and let it push through us.

To ignore these sweaty concepts creates more pain and allows for more destruction. Think about climate change. We all hope that technology will solve all the problems we've made. We'll somehow just make enough renewable energy and sequester enough carbon. But to pretend that capitalism is going to clean up its own mess is a misplaced hope. It's naïve.

To drown in the sorrow doesn't help either. You still have to be able to play.

In a way, scuba diving is deeply bracketing. The whole world goes away. In other ways, it's more vast than anything.

So much of our everyday (air-filled, land-based) world disappears when we enter the water. We can't see as far under-water. Hearing works differently. Sight changes. The world expands to everything while also contracting to the small space around you.

Bracketing lets you play. It can allow you to see what's already there and delight in it. True play best exists outside of expectations—of what it should be, of what it could be.

Bracketing out expectations gives you adventure. Not adventure in the sense of white men discovering places already inhabited. A wilder one.

The limits of bracketing give you the freedom of experience. It lets you sink into relaxation.

Sometimes I wish I could bracket out sounds. The loud, man-made ones that make me want to crawl into the fetal position or cry in the corner. They melt my synapses. I hold my breath as a way to hide in place, and eczema erupts across my body. I don't relax.

A manta slapping its large body on the ocean's surface or an unexpected lion's roar too close doesn't do this to me. (I know this for a fact.) Those types of sounds don't overload my brain like the screech of a subway can. Nor does much else out there in wilderness—land or sea—deluge my brain in that way.

In a pool I have to work hard to feel meditative in the experience. An ocean makes it easy.

There's just something different about how my brain feels when I'm outdoors for long periods of time.

Even when we're having some serious Type II fun, the vastness works its magic on us. Frank Hurley, the Australian photographer who frequently went on expeditions to Antarctica, understood this. He wrote, "After life in the vastness of a vacant continent, civilisation seemed disappointingly narrow, cramped, superficial and empty. A couple of weeks it sufficed to bring on an attack of wander fever."

Hurley collectively spent four years in Antarctica on various expeditions, including the 1914–1917 Shackleton expedition where their boat, the *Endurance*, got trapped in ice floats and slowly sank. Against incredible odds, all humans aboard that ship returned to England alive (the dogs didn't). They sailed tiny lifeboats, ate seals and penguins, and while the rest stayed in a rock shelter on an uninhabited island, four of them got to civilization by climbing mountain routes still barely accessible to professional mountaineers today—all with pretty basic gear and before the widespread use of two-way radio.

And yet, Hurley preferred it to the crampedness of city streets. Not because he was some misanthrope, but rather he understood that there's magic in those vast spaces. It's a magic we're too often missing in our everyday lives.

The vastness of wilderness—even a dense jungle or a strong current underwater—lets my brain relax.

When relaxed, I notice more. I see (and hear) the line blur between human-created and nature. That binary doesn't feel so rigid. Diverse takeout cuisines and functioning public transportation are not in opposition to healthy wildernesses. You can have it all—just not in the same place.

Play happens in all spaces. Adventure is a silly and delightful form of play.

When you play, delights appear often. I'd bet a lot of money that most, if not all, species on earth play. We maybe just don't know what to look for when we watch their activity out in the field doing research. When other species play like we play, we see it.

Beyond the mirror test, it's clear mantas play. They play in ways similar to us, similar to our pets. Even in heightened moments of excited play, mantas can look so calm as they glide. I wonder if, like us, they ever get pissy at one another. Not the usual "you've stolen my mate or territory" we usually assign to animals as the only rationale for their anger. But rather a bad mood, having woken up on the wrong side of the bed, annoyance.

We know mantas can dive to depths farther than we can track and recognize themselves in a mirror. We don't know if they ever snap at one another, saying, "Can you just fucking not flap your wings like that today, Bob? You're really getting on my last nerve." I'd like to imagine that they do.

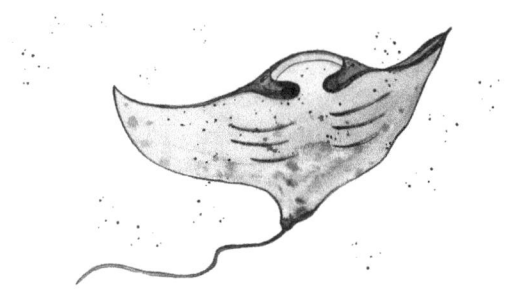

Chapter 5

Feminism in the Similans

I enjoy being surprised by the weird things underwater on a dive. Once, on a night dive in the Similans in Thailand, an eel spooked me by coming from behind me, over my shoulder, and in front of my face to look straight at me before meandering on. It was delightful.

Someone who also spent a lot of life noticing was Robert Byron. He was a British travel writer who adventured across India, Tibet, Russia, Afghanistan, and more—before dying at thirty-five in World War II. His writing style, steeped in his colonialist education in history, tends to reflect a deep curiosity about the world. He wrote, "The supreme moments of travel are born of beauty and strangeness in equal parts: the first panders to the senses, the second to the mind; and it is the rarity of this coincidence which makes the rarity of these moments."

Instead of eels checking me out, I'm usually the one looking out for the strange things underwater—like a frogfish. It's a fish the size of your palm, uses its fins to seemingly walk on the ground, and has the cutest, grumpiest scowl of a face.

The duality of strangeness and beauty that Byron found traveling is amplified underwater. One of my favorite examples is nudibranchs (pronounced: noodi-brank-s), tiny shell-less mollusks that come in every neon color imaginable and possess both male and female sex organs. Some can even photosynthesize after eating algae.

Most underwater creatures are this way—strange and beautiful. Even the ones whose names we all know how to pronounce. Jellyfish don't have a brain and are 95 percent water—but can somehow hunt prey. We're not exactly sure how they do that. Octopuses, on the other hand, have nine brains. One in their head, the others are each in an arm. These brains seemingly coordinate but act independently from one another. That's helpful because they're all squish, no bones. The only hard part of an octopus's body is the beak found inside its mouth.

For me, part of the reason diving seems so freeing is that it feels like traveling to an alternate universe—where brains matter and don't. Everything is just so strange underwater. Creatures look different than how I know them to look above water.

Above-water rules—like plants and animals are distinct— blur underwater. Take coral, for example. They're both a plant and an animal—and they kinda look like clusters of pretty rocks. Some coral is over 4,000 years old (it's deepwater black coral found off the coast of Hawaii).

Less old but still very spectacular coral is found all over the waters of Thailand. One of my favorite places within Thailand is the Similans. The Similans are an archipelago of nine uninhabited islands in the Thailand part of the Andaman Sea. The best way to dive this region is by liveaboard (as is true of most good dive spots) that leave from Khao Lak. It's a great place to see weird things—big and small.

It was a wee bit stormy when I went to the Similans. The water's surface had rolling waves and stiff winds. Below the surface was calm, albeit with strong currents that whipped us around—and swirled the marine life.

As the adventurer Kate Harris writes, "Give me storms and scurvy any day over a slow, pale death by computer screen and Diet Coke."

When the conditions are less than perfect, you need to closely consider your options for entering the water with your scuba gear. Maybe you roll backward off a dingy. Perhaps you ungainly walk from the beach in your fins and slowly swim to the shore reef. Or, my favorite, you do a step-jump off the back of a boat—it's basically a giant stride into the ocean where you enter the water vertically, feet first.

Usually, the giant stride is the most fun way to enter the water—you're leaping into the ocean. It's also the safest when there are stormy waves. What's not fun is when those large waves are wildly rocking the liveaboard boat, so you mistime your stride, face-planting horizontally into the ocean with heavy scuba gear on. Not that I would know anything about that type of ungraceful entrance—or that I did that multiple times on the same trip.

When it's stormy on the surface like that, you get straight to sinking down into the ocean—and don't have time to think too much about your bruised ego or face. On a calmer day, everyone might enter the water from the boat, hang out at the surface, chat and make sure everything is good before descending. Not in rolling waves or strong currents—you need to descend safely but quickly.

If you take too long descending—because you're slowly equalizing your ears or fiddling with unknown gear— the current will pull you away from the rest of your dive group. Remember: Diving is just physics. The current's strength changes at different depths. It will (usually) pull you harder at the surface than it will thirty feet down. You want your whole dive group to be pulled by the same current strength—to be on the same aquatic equivalent of an airport moving sidewalk. You don't want to be at the surface, speeding along, when everyone else is waiting deeper, slowly plodding.

Having the right gear—and being well-versed in it—helps you dive in more-technical situations. It enables you to show up to complex conditions and have fun.

Scuba diving often gets quite cold. At least where I like to go, in strong, cold currents. The above-water temperature might be warm, but below water is frigid.

A semi-thick wetsuit helps keep your body warmish during the dive. I finally bought my own after too many dives in too large wetsuits. Well-fitted, a wetsuit hugs you tight, adding millimeters of neoprene to hold in your body heat. When a wetsuit is too large, you almost might as well not wear it—cold water easily flows between your body and the suit, cooling your body down.

Ill-fitting technical adventure gear is a problem I often run into—not just in diving. Many women do. Luckily, the past decade has seen a wonderful proliferation of by-women, for-women gear and adventure clothing, making this somewhat less of a problem. I may not find well-fitting gear at a random dive shop like Sam, who is a six-foot-tall, average-built male, can. But at least I can find it on the internet at home and bring it with me around the world.

Even with a properly fitting wetsuit, I need to warm back up after a dive. The most delightful way to do this is to change quickly into a dry bathing suit and then sit with a cup of tea on the boat's deck in the warm, tropical sun.

Diving from a liveaboard forces these downtimes between dives. You physically can only dive for so long and must wait prescribed times between dives. So you sit on the boat's deck and watch the open ocean, warming yourself up and remembering the magical world beneath the water's surface.

That's the point of diving, this popping down into the unknown and playing there. Other adventurers understand this type of rigorous enjoyment. George Mallory, the British mountaineer who attempted to climb Mount Everest three times in the 1920s (and eventually died on the mountain), wrote: "People ask me, 'What is the use of climbing Mount Everest?' and my answer must at once be, 'It is of no use.' There is not the slightest prospect of any gain whatsoever. . . . What we get from this adventure is just sheer joy. And joy is, after all, the end of life."

In much the same way as mountaineering, diving is utterly freeing and completely limited. It's a paradox. Underwater, if you avoid acknowledging your limitations, death will easily, speedily arrive. But spend the whole time monitoring your depth, oxygen levels, and precise location? No, that'd miss the whole point of existence—and scuba diving in beautiful spots. The freedom and joy of scuba diving is looking at the weird shit underwater. The point of it is to enter an alternate reality.

Diving always makes me think of Simone de Beauvoir, who spent so much of her life thinking and writing about the paradoxical existence of human freedom and external constraints. You can live however you want—except that you kinda can't. Life becomes more interesting when you pretend you can and nod only occasionally to limitations.

Beauvoir believed such freedom and constraints continually help us become ourselves in the world. As she wrote about making choices, a choice is "constantly in the making; it is repeated every time that I become conscious of it."

We can see in Beauvoir's journals and notes that she dealt with these intensely sweaty concepts for much of her life, starting when she was very young. To get at these concepts, she'd often ask herself questions in her notes: "Become who you are? Do you know yourself? Do you see yourself?"

Sara Ahmed echoes this sentiment when she writes: "To live a feminist life is to make everything into something that is questionable. The question of how to live a feminist life is alive as a question as well as being a life question."

We ask questions. We make choices. We do not come into the world fully formed. The world shapes us. We shape ourselves. As Beauvoir famously argued, one is not born a woman but becomes one. (Later, she added that this is true of men, too. If she were alive today, I think she'd expand it to all forms of gender expression.)

We are continually becoming who we are through our actions, the ferocity with which we approach our freedoms, and the ways we live with our contingencies. We constantly make choices as to how to live. It's terrifying and rewarding.

Above water, the contingencies of life—including the usual gendered bullshit—can be hard to ignore. (It's easier to ignore sexism—and all the other isms—when all you can hear underwater is the sound of your out-gassed air bubbles.) Once after a dive in a different part of Thailand, an idiot dude kept asking the woman working as the boat's divemaster what she did in "real life." Her face immediately showed an annoyance I think all women have felt. She paused for a few beats before answering "Uhhh, this is my real life."

He wouldn't take that as an answer and instead kept questioning, saying, "No, no. What do you *do*?"

Like many service professions, guides in the outdoors make a substantial amount of their income off tips. You could see the divemaster doing the calculations that so many other women in similar jobs do: Do I tell him to fuck off—I'm literally working at my job right now—and risk losing his tip? Or, do I get this conversation over with and hopefully still get paid?

She, understandably so, chose the latter option. She said, "I used to be a veterinarian." That did the trick and he left her alone, free from what he likely thought was casual small talk. In his mind, I'm sure he almost meant it like a compliment—*I had such an amazing time on this dive, but this isn't my everyday reality. It, thus, can't be your daily reality. What is your everyday reality?*

He didn't pester the men working on the boat like this.

It was unpleasant to witness—and a much more mundane version of the gendering that can happen in these spaces. Fragile masculinity abounds everywhere but especially in outdoor spaces. Adventuring is so much more interesting and joyful than that bullshit—for everyone.

The outdoors—and adventuring in general—has never been the sole domain of non-disabled, white men who can afford fancy gear. That rhetoric is political, purposeful, stupid, historically inaccurate, and dumb. Those types of men are, of course, welcome in the outdoors, but theirs is not the only story of adventures and of finding pleasure in goofing around in nature. Or, of working in nature.

This man was a great example of the many unsure-of-themselves men in these outdoor spaces: He had a ton of new equipment and talked too big of a game about previous dive trips.

I've rarely seen a woman do this. I've seen countless dudes show up to a dive with expensive equipment they don't know how to use. I've heard so many men brag about how deep they dove on previous trips, unaware that's completely not the point of scuba diving.

Honestly, it's a nice red flag: Any man who brags about how deep he has dived will be a terrible (probably inexperienced) diver, unable to control his buoyancy underwater, and should be given a lot of room so that he doesn't careen into you.

I understand the humanity behind the brags and unnecessary purchases. It's hiding fear. The bragging often comes across as convincing themselves they're up for the task of the dive as much as it is to impress others. The purchases seem to express a form of excitement performed through capitalism. I, too, love new toys and planning what equipment I'm going to bring on a trip.

The problem is how much space this can take up on an adventure—figuratively and literally. It'd be much easier if these types of men could just say, "I'm slightly afraid of the dive we're about to do but also very excited"—that'd be a lot more enjoyable for everyone involved. Instead, the conversations they force steamroll others, often women.

Physically, these types of new toys underwater can be ungainly. Diving with something like a large camera requires deeply understanding buoyancy and your position in space. That way you don't hurt yourself or other creatures by diving distractedly, potentially bumping into fragile things, like coral, or grabbing poisonous things, like the venomous rockfish, which easily can be mistaken for a good rock to pinch and steady yourself underwater.

It requires an ability to use the new toy while also maintaining an awareness of your surroundings. It's all too easy to hyper-focus on some piece of gear to the detriment of seeing what there is to see underwater. You might miss the remarkable creatures of the oceans. But, you might also not see your oxygen levels dropping or a somewhat dangerous animal you need to keep half an eye on.

As I see it, if we're to walk this tightrope of constraint and freedom for the entirety of our lives, we might as well channel Mallory's understanding that joy is the point. We can feel overwhelmed by this paradox or play in it. The difference is found in how we understand the word freedom.

Sara Maitland, whose work on the inner ghost undermining our alone time I mentioned in Chapter 2, has spent a long time thinking about the types of freedom that exist. She writes, "Freedom has two dimensions: there is 'freedom from'—the things you dislike, that bind or limit you (poverty, pain or fear, for example). And there is 'freedom to,' which is, I think, the more important, the more joyful and the more enriching."

A prerequisite of this "freedom to" is a vulnerability that requires long periods of undistracted existence. You need the mental space to craft that vulnerability—as well as the physical space to protect that mental space. There's a reason Virginia Woolf's *A Room of Her Own* continues to resonate with women today.

Such space lets you understand things. Pick out the signal from the noise to listen without being overwhelmed.

It allows you to see what requires your attention. As Beauvoir wrote, "There is no divorce between philosophy and life. Every living step is a philosophical choice."

On land, it feels as if we act on a physical space, not within it. A dive underwater forces you to recognize that you move through space. Water forces you to follow its own rules and patterns. Bracing against the flow does not help. Float with it. Is floating the same as not bracing against? Or is it more than that? It is not bracing against but also something more . . . going with things? When you float, aren't you floating with or on something?

We do so much to avoid floating along with our lives. We seek to constantly occupy our brains to stave off boredom, the periods of silence that go with it, and the thoughts that rush in to fill that silence. The pause often scares us. Too often, boredom gets viewed as an absence of something rather than a way to wander. We seek "freedom from" instead of "freedom to," as Maitland would say.

It's easy to forget these nuances of freedom. We can get caught up in the limitations and ignore not just the nuances but the whole concept of freedom altogether. In the short term of life, it's much easier not to be vulnerable. (Long term—different story.) Uncertainty feels icky. It is uncomfortable. I'm not sure anyone actually likes it. There's a reason Kirkegaard wrote that "anxiety is the dizziness of freedom."

Maybe certain individuals have a higher threshold for it than others. Perhaps some like more spontaneity in life than others. I know I have phases where I crave spontaneity and other periods where I'd love if everything could be known.

Uncertainty feels different from unknowing. Uncertainty lives in a murky middle between known and unknown. You have just enough of both to have neither.

Any adventurer can confirm: Mental rigidity kills. It kills the fun, too. Plans are only best guesses. So are ontological paradigms. Travel makes me want to travel more. I would like to revisit everywhere I've been and explore where I haven't. Each book read leads me to new ones. Why presume an end?

Tidied structures of the world's sweaty concepts—and brags about ourselves—give us helpful illusions. But they're just that.

That's why uncertainty can feel icky. You are aware that you reside somewhat in the unknowing—that there's just so much you don't know. As Virginia Woolf, who could portray the inner life of a human better than probably anyone else, wrote, "To speak of knowledge is futile. All is experiment and adventure. We are forever mixing ourselves with unknown quantities."

You have to be brave enough to play, to let yourself indulge in good nonsense and enjoy life. This is true for all genders and can be hard no matter your gender. It is powerful to prioritize recreation, adventure, and fun. It is a different mindset from prioritizing what you think you *should* be doing. Doing adventure, whatever that means, requires listening to yourself and the things that bring you joy—as well as the next step: following what you hear, even if that leads you into completely unknown things.

Sara Ahmed uses the word *hap* to explore life's unknowing. Hap, an archaic word I needed to look up, can be used as both a noun and verb. As a noun, it means luck or fortune. As a verb, it means to come about by chance.

Hap is how I found diving. I meandered to northern Thailand and then kept wandering south. Hap is how I do most things in life. In fear, I can easily overplan. But, if you let them, usually plans take a left turn—for the better.

As Ahmed explains about hap: "Once I found the word, I fell for it. When I go for a walk without knowing where I am going, I call it a hap walk. To affirm hap is to follow a queer route: you are not sure which way you are going; maybe you let your feet decide for you. You can be redirected by what you encounter along the way as you are not rushing ahead, rushing forward, to get somewhere. You wander, haphazardly at times, but then you might acquire a sense of purpose because of what you find on the way. How we take a walk is not unrelated to how we live a life. To proceed without assuming there is a right direction is to proceed differently."

That's why each of us, together and separately, claiming our authentic lives and joys on meandering hap walks matters.

The more you grapple with sweaty concepts and live how you want to live, the easier it is for me to realize that is true for me too. Together we can help one another walk our own paths.

Had I not taken a hap walk into uncertainty and learned to dive, I would have missed out on this strange activity that brings me to alternate universes and a floating freedom. We all have similar examples in our own lives. What if we hadn't ventured into that coffee shop that morning? Or chatted with that interesting stranger? What if we hadn't wandered into that beautiful park to look at the pretty flowers across the way? So much of what we value in life arises out of these accidental happenings.

Beauvoir understood this uncertainty paradox—physically and mentally walking between constraint and freedom lets us have more alive lives. Hap lets us do what Virginia Woolf did so well: notice the world.

Sometimes what you notice on a dive is what I call the blue void. It happens when all you can see is the deep blue ocean in all directions — a trippy existence where space, time, and direction melt away. Tie yourself to your breath, to the entire ocean with its blue that seems to go on forever. Match your breathing to the slow rhythms of the world without unwittingly meandering up too high towards the surface or too deep. You feel both utterly alone as you look into the blue void and wholly connected to everything else in the universe.

It's completive but also fun. It's playing in the unknown.

Mostly, one's interactions with the blue void happen during safety stops. In the Similans, like many dive spots, you do most of your safety stops out in the open ocean, not near any of the oceanic landmarks you've spent your time diving nearby. As you wait the three minutes at five meters for your body to off-gas the accumulated nitrogen, you hang out in what feels like outer space.

During a safety stop you float, attached to nothing except the other humans nearby and the numbers on your dive watch that tell you how deep you are in the ocean. Without those little numbers, it's incredibly easy to float up or sink down large distances without realizing it—something quite dangerous underwater if done unintentionally.

With a dive watch and the others diving with you, you've got a safety net. Some like to use blue void safety stops to practice their buoyancy—watching closely their watch's depth measurements as they try to not move too far up or down while breathing normally. I like to use that safety net to look out into the blue void of the open ocean.

Shackleton understood this need to look out into the void. He wrote: "Men go out into the void spaces of the world for various reasons. Some are actuated simply by a love of adventure, some have the keen thirst for scientific knowledge, and others again are drawn away from the trodden paths by the 'lure of little voices,' the mysterious fascination of the unknown."

The fascination of the unknown is true for us women too, even if Shackleton wouldn't let any come on his expeditions. (I have always felt a kinship with the women who applied for his expeditions.)

Floating in the blue void, you see only blue. All directions—up, down, left, right. I always hope some big creature will come careening out of the void, heading at us. (How cool would that be to have a giant shark or whale pop out of nowhere?) So far that hasn't happened. Instead, I'm left with wondering in awe at the spaciousness of our world.

Michael Harris, a Canadian journalist, wrote a lovely book about solitude, his own relationship to it and our larger cultural understandings of it. Solitude and wild spaces often go together in our cultural lexicon. As Harris writes about the importance of going to wild spaces: "We become little bodies in a very big world and egos shrink accordingly."

Remembering how small we are lets us better engage with the large world we inhabit. It allows us to have boundaries and thus better adventure. We can prioritize true relaxation over mindless internet scrolling. We can slowly remove ourselves from the state of half-panic too many of us inhabit: never fully overloaded, never fully relaxed. Too often we're always somewhat in panic mode but not in complete panic mode. We don't know what constitutes an emergency anymore—nor rest. And we too easily forget what play feels like.

I think it is a crucial step (and one that ought to be often repeated) for living an engaged life. You can't do real recreation—or adventure—without remembering how large the universe is and how comparatively tiny we all are. That remembering gives us freedom.

Chapter 6

Fear in Sipadan

As with all dives, the point of a night dive is to chill out and look at all the cool things: the weird, the beautiful, the ugly, the slightly scary, and everything else. You float along, able to see only the world illuminated by your flashlight and the flashlights of others nearby. You inch around in this existence, moving slowly and purposely.

You move with purpose because if sand gets stirred up—by you, another human, or a creature disturbed—you get enveloped in a fog of particles swirling around you. (It feels like being enveloped by a universe's worth of glittering stars.) Your sense of place in space becomes lost. You become unmoored. (And, that's if you're already paying attention to your location.)

Time and space become fuzzier in the dark. Visual distances shrink and expand according much more to mindset than feet and inches. Your destination, be it a dive boat or the occasional retrofitted oil rig, is never far away. But it often feels like a different world, especially in the dark. As if you need to first cross the universe before the dive is done.

In that dreamy headspace, where you end and the universe begins is unclear. The world seems big. It feels full of potential. Who knows what you'll find.

Sharks, more active at night, look at you with catlike eyes. The universe around you fills up with colorful lobsters, glowing plankton, roaming octopuses, fish you've maybe never seen before, and moray eels that glide out of nowhere with their cute noses and awkward teeth. Colors, too, are richer on a night dive.

Our eyes' ability to see certain colors fades the deeper you go underwater. Different colors' wavelengths get absorbed differently by the water. We lose the reds first. Then oranges and yellows. A flashlight can add brilliance back to our perception of the scenery and creatures. The light doesn't have to travel from the surface down. Instead, it's coming from your flashlight. That means you can better see the full spectrum of colors present underwater. The underwater rainbow of colors is contrasted against the pitch black, which is everything not lit up by your light, seemingly heightening the intensity of colors you can see.

How I often feel on night dives is similar to what Sara Wheeler wrote in *Terra Incognita*: "It was the purest landscape, the grandest, and so it seemed to me, the most exalted. I had a powerful sense that I didn't exist at all. The sublime grandeur of nature can strip away layers of the ego—I had experienced it once in the Australian outback, lying under an immense purple sky as the heat rose off the sun-cooked earth."

Most often on night dives I feel curiosity instead of fear. The world seems intangibly big. There's so much of interest to be seen in the small beam of my flashlight and yet also so much unknown out there in the black darkness. Sure, maybe there's a giant monster a bit out of sight. Probably not. Likely, if there is a large creature nearby it is looking for dinner—and I'm not dinner.

As the anthropologist Loren Eiseley, who died in 1977 and was best known for his ability to write poems to explain scientific concepts, wrote, "If there is magic on this planet, it is contained in water." Whenever you dive, but especially if you dive at night, you've traveled to another universe and eventually surface back into this universe but changed. Always changed.

Unless you're doing an exploratory dive, most dives have a right place to surface and a mentally mapped route to follow. That's for safety—things like deadly underwater whirlpools are best avoided. If it's a well-known spot, it's also for showcasing the places where the cool creatures reside and the best coral exists. And it's for convenience. If you're diving off of a boat, you want to surface relatively close to that boat. Currents can be strong on the surface. Waves and wind add unexpected challenges.

If everything is okay, the slow meander from that wrong location back to the boat is one of my favorite things about diving. It's a movement that feels incredibly graceful. If I look anything like every other diver covering distance on the ocean's surface, it's a distinctly ungraceful, awkward swim-float-waddle.

Moving gracefully underwater with gear is easy—not so easy on the surface.

If the distance between where you were supposed to surface and where you actually are is far, you rearrange your gear. You switch things up so that the floaty, air-filled bits lay under your stomach (as opposed to on your back). This way lets you doggy-paddle, supported by an inflated dive vest.

But if it isn't that far and the time not urgent, I like to not reorganize my gear but instead float-swim on my back, steadily fluttering my fins. A float-swim on your back takes a lot longer to get anywhere. You're almost guaranteed not to go in a straight line. Why hurry out of an ocean's water if not necessary?

You'd think that after a night dive this would be kinda scary. All you see of your boat is distant lights—and those lights might not be where you'd thought they'd be.

But I enjoy it. I like to float-swim on my back after most all night dives, not just the ones where I've surfaced in an unintended location. (There's always a bit of distance to be covered, even if you've hit your intended surfacing mark.) As I flutter my fins and slowly meander, the sky full of stars and the ocean filled with sparkling water become confused in my head.

Quick or harsh movements don't work well with dive gear. Instead: Glide through space. With the stars above you reflected in the inky dark water around you, it feels like you're in outer space.

Paul Theroux, the grumpiest travel writer to perhaps have ever existed, understood this beauty (while still acknowledging that sometimes people are the worst, travel is uncomfortable, and everything is stupid). During his eighteen-month travels around Oceania in a folding kayak (following a separation from his wife), Theroux wrote about the beautiful disorientation of sky and sea at night under the stars: "I especially recalled how one day sailing back to an island we were delayed, and night fell. There were stars everywhere, above us, and reflected in the sea along with the sparkle of phosphorescence streaming from the bow wave. When I poked an oar in the ocean and stirred it, the sea glittered with twinkling sea life. We sped onwards. There were no lights on shore. It was as though we were in an old rickety rocket ship."

I was excited to dive the Sipadan region at night. Jacques Cousteau, the famous oceanographer and filmmaker, called Sipadan an "untouched piece of art." Night diving heightens the otherworldliness of the ocean, so I couldn't wait to see how this piece of art looked with splashes of bioluminescence, prowling nocturnal creatures, and total darkness beyond my light.

It's in a region—Sabah, Malaysia—where the above-water beauty is only surpassed by what you can see below water. It's got almost everything one would want to see: high mountains, dense jungles, stunning beaches, open ocean, and healthy coral. The region is teeming with biodiversity.

I've been there a couple of times to visit the world-renowned dive spots and hike in the rainforests. Sipadan, my favorite place in Sabah, is a specific island within the remote dive region, but the diving area itself is also colloquially known as Sipadan.

I usually find out about good dive spots by asking dive professionals about their favorites. Sipadan kept coming up over and over. I went there and immediately understood.

The region is so popular that the Malaysian government strictly limits the number of people allowed to dive at specific dive spots each day and even what time of day you can dive those spots. Only certain spots are "open" at night—for a good reason, as I'd later learn.

The Sipadan area has healthy corals of all colors, an abundance of turtles and sharks, vast schools of *hundreds* of barracudas that will sometimes swirl rapidly around you, and the clearest, light blue water with visibility that seems to reach into infinity. There are so many cool things to see—and seemingly never-ending visibility with which to see it. It's literally diving heaven. There's a good reason many recount that quote by Cousteau.

On a later trip after this one, Sipadan is where I brought Sam to learn how to scuba dive. I wanted him to love it as much as I do and so stacked the deck in my favor by having him first dive at one of the best spots in the world. It worked—I now have a dive buddy in Sam, who loves diving and is as good as I am.

Sipadan is technically an intermediate to advanced dive region because of its shifty and strong currents. Sam is a strong athlete with a calm temperament, so I figured he could handle it. (He could.) I also didn't mention ahead of time that it was a more intense dive region than most. Instead, I sold it on the barracuda swirls, the sleepy sharks, and the colorful corals. I wouldn't necessarily recommend learning at Sipadan to everyone, especially if the open ocean freaks you out. But, as in Sam's case, if you learn on more intense dives—and learn good current technique from the start—later dives seem easy in comparison.

The region has two accommodation options: a single hotel on an island and an offshore refurbished, decommissioned oil rig with a hotel on top and a house reef underneath.

A house reef is like a house garden—except it's underwater. It's a catchall term for a reef easily accessible and protected from strong waves and currents. Often you'll find them in front of fancy resorts, advertised as great snorkeling destinations. If the resort is lucky, the reef just happened to be there. Usually—like with a home garden—someone has planted and cultivated the reef, hoping cool fish come and visit, just like you plant specific flowers for butterflies, bees, and hummingbirds.

Coral scientists have developed underwater metal structures that baby coral can be attached to and (hopefully) safely grow. With enough baby coral and time, you have a flourishing coral garden. It looks like a tidy English garden underwater.

You can attract even more creatures if you're a bit less particular about aesthetics. One of the easiest ways to plant coral is by anchoring it to a preexisting structure, like industrial human trash. Crashed airplanes, sunken boats, abandoned oil rigs—these left-behind trash don't decompose easily. Just like on land when a forest eventually takes over an abandoned house, with moss growing on the walls, trees sprouting through the floor, and vines crawling in the windows, so too will the ocean grow over abandoned structures underwater.

This isn't to say that we should litter or abandon oil rigs (or even be looking for oil in the oceans), but that this weird thing happens in oceans all over the place. Some of the most interesting, human-curated dive sites are literally large pieces of trash, accidentally or on purpose becoming a beautiful safe haven for reefs and fish.

It makes for some sweaty concept-thinking while diving: You float, enjoying looking at some of the most beautiful underwater creatures growing on something (an oil rig) so iconically terrible for both the immediate flora and fauna as well as the entirety of our planet.

On an immediate level, no matter how much coral might be flourishing on it, a decommissioned oil rig or a crashed airplane or a sunken ship is still a very large piece of trash. And trash that's found in a marine wilderness with little human industrial impact. What's in that trash (oils, chemicals, asbestos, etc.) may also be killing or changing the very coral that's growing on it.

Plus, you know, oil rigs and airplane emissions directly contribute to greenhouse gasses, one of the major factors of mass coral die-off.

And yet, there's a beauty in it. A tinge of hope that maybe the future is this: oil replaced by renewables, corals growing instead of dying.

Night scuba diving can be amazing and also terrifying. It's like digging into a sweaty concept. You get turned around quickly. It feels like you're moving faster than you are (like running at night—you believe you're flying, sprinting with no effort). That's fun. You can get absorbed into minute details you'd otherwise ignore in the daytime. But it also means that your sense of time and space disappears—or at least radically alters.

Even in the dreamy headspace that comes after a dive, I am still aware of something the novelist Jhumpa Lahiri once wrote: "But you can't float without the possibility of drowning, of sinking." To float on the surface is not to sink. To drown is not achieving that float and staying too long discombobulated underwater. It's a tradeoff risk I'm familiar with and often unafraid of.

I try hard not to get complacent diving, but it happens. When I make that kind of mistake, it usually results in a terrifying situation, like getting lost underwater in a strong current at night, where if you can't make it back to safety, you might just float out to the open ocean, never to be seen again—that is, if you make it to the surface safely with enough oxygen.

I'm not theorizing here. I once found myself in that completely avoidable situation in Sipadan.

I got lost underwater because the dive itself was easy—I forgot I was in the wilderness. With two others, I was diving on the house reef below the oil rig we were staying on. It wasn't the crazy dive sites of the region. It wasn't with scary, gigantic creatures. It was mundane and pleasant. It was the diving equivalent of doing a garden tour at someone's house—just underwater—and getting terribly lost. It's more than slightly embarrassing to get lost on such a dive.

It was so mundane and pleasant of a dive that we made a classic, by-the-book complacency mistake that can prove deadly in all adventure activities: We didn't communicate enough before we dove. Each of us assumed another person was leading the dive and responsible for paying attention to our location underwater.

In the daytime, that wouldn't have caused any problems. The visibility is so clear that you can almost always see the oil rig's legs and orient yourself on this house reef dive. It'd be the most leisurely dive with a pinch of paying attention and clear communication. Darkness complicates things.

You can't easily communicate in the dark underwater. Nothing is visible beyond the beam of your flashlight. If you turn off your light (or the battery dies) you won't be able to see nor will you be visible to other divers. Sometimes you wear a rave party glow stick hanging off your dive gear so that others can find you if your light turns off and you're not too far away. To gesture—the primary form of communication underwater—you shine your light at yourself.

Almost immediately into the dive, I got turned around. I'm not someone who can navigate by cardinal directions. I go off landmarks. (That means swirly routes are where I shine and that I can get lost in a gridded city.) You can't see landmarks in the dark while diving. I wasn't worried though—I wasn't the one leading the dive. Or so I thought.

An embarrassingly long time passed before we three did the underwater equivalent of "Why are you following me? I'm following you. Oh fuck."

It involved lots of frantic hand signals lit up by our flashlights and attempts at facial expressions behind dive masks.

We tried to look for other divers' flashlights glowing in the distance with no luck. All we could see was what glowed in the light of our flashlights. Everything else was pitch black.

The refurbished oil rig we were diving under was no longer above us. I realized it had been a while since I had seen one of its legs jutting down into the seafloor.

We spent around thirty seconds vainly trying to locate a landmark or one of the oil rig legs with our flashlights. A landmark could have grounded us to the larger context, to the map we had in our heads. Once you're off, it's hard to get back on a map.

Part of the reason the dive area is so unique is its remoteness. You need to fly to Semporna in East Sabah, Malaysia—a tiny corner of Malaysian Borneo with no direct flights from any major hub—then get onto a boat that will ferry you to either that single hotel on an island or the oil rig with the house reef below.

On the boat ride out to the dive spots, you pass some of the ocean-based villages of the Sama-Bajau. They're nomadic seafaring peoples who live on houseboats that float in the water, from which they free dive for fun, food, and a way of life.

As with most nomadic peoples these days, the regional governments are increasingly making it hard to live as the Sama-Bajau have historically done—without nation-state identities and fluidly crossing such borders. There are estimated to be over a million people who identify as Sama-Bajau, mostly living in the Philippines, Malaysia, Indonesia, and Brunei.

Passing a floating village cluster, you feel the remoteness of the region. Other human habitations can't be seen in any direction—and the Sama-Bajau villages appear and disappear from sight rather quickly as you pass them in the speedboat.

Which is to say: Sipadan is out there.

If you're lost at sea here, you might just be lost forever. At least it certainly felt that way when I started to panic when I realized we were lost diving the house reef.

This dive was a house garden. It wasn't a dangerous environment. The currents were gentle. No scary creatures. Nothing dramatic. And yet, I just felt really afraid. I felt really lost.

We've all felt this way before—lost and disoriented. It happens even when we're not out on the open ocean or in a wetsuit. We're (metaphorically) shining our lights around and just can't locate ourselves. We feel untethered and adrift. It can happen in the office or classroom as easily as it can in the ocean. A little voice in our head whispers, *What the fuck am I doing?*

It's easy to lose your nerve if you overthink things—a million things about why you can't pop into your brain. I tell myself it's too much, too big. Or the reverse: I'm too small, too weak. It isn't true. It is a very convenient lie to keep me stuck, feeling practical about my choices.

For most people, bopping around in the open ocean at night would be the scariest area of nature. For me, it's the near-shore, where waves crash into sand and thrash me about.

Relaxing in those crashing ocean waves landing on the shore—as opposed to riding underwater currents—requires an inner calm, confidence, and physicality that I'd often prefer to pretend not to have. I know I have it in underwater currents or on long-distance hikes. But in the land-meets-ocean chaos, it can be easier for me to be paralyzed by fear, to be afraid of getting into the waves, than to take some deep breaths, realize I'm fine, and go play.

Another water environment that freaks me out is shipwreck diving. I don't play inside those structures. Shipwrecks are slowly being broken down by the ocean. I have no interest in an off-kilter kick from another diver (or myself) accidentally accelerating that breakdown and bringing the whole ship crashing down while we're inside it. Or getting caught on something or lost inside a structure without a clear and easy exit to the surface. Sure, maybe I'll look at them from the outside, but it's never very fun. Usually, if I'm looking at a shipwreck, I'm wondering where the bodies are—and if they were removed to make it a tourist attraction.

All of our fears aren't just getting crushed by a shipwreck underwater or floating adrift out into the open ocean. We panic over tests, what someone else might think of us, something dumb we said, what job we should do, not feeling good enough, not being certain about the future . . . and seemingly everything else.

Sometimes it helps to remember that unfamiliar doesn't always mean lost. Sometimes you're not lost. You're just seeing it from a different perspective.

This happens to me when I'm driving on roads at home all the time. I'm really sure I've never been here before and have no idea which street to turn down to get home. Sometimes I have been there. Other times, I actually am in a new place.

Maybe what I'm not is lost. Just outside the lines of comfort and familiarity. Remote—but in a good way. Too little fear leads you to underestimate the potentially deadly forces of nature, to forget to be humble. Too much fear and you miss out on an adventure.

It's a situation that isn't asking for panic. Instead, it's asking you to expand your vision, your sense of where you are, your orientation—how you view everything. It's asking not for a freakout but a sense of wonder at exploring something new.

Eventually, amid feeling lost and freaking out about it, something reorients you and everything clicks. You remember why you're in graduate school, how to navigate this type of work project, or what to do when lost at sea (or lost while driving). When we find ourselves, we all can feel dumb at those times. It's a real humbling moment of *oh yeah, I know how to do this, how to handle this—the panic is silly.* Even when that panic felt extremely un-silly just seconds before.

During that disorienting house reef dive somehow—I don't quite remember—someone suggested that we head in one direction for a bit, hoping it would lead us back to where we had just come from. It didn't work. We turned around and started slowly heading towards what we thought was back.

In the dark it's easy to go in circles thinking you're going straight.

We were all hyperaware of our oxygen consumption at this point. I checked mine constantly and could see the other two's flashlights often beaming at their oxygen readers.

That's the thing about getting lost underwater: Your oxygen supply is limited. When I was lost in thought in Copenhagen, for example, I never had to worry about drowning or drifting away into the unknown high seas on the surface. My fear during this time was much more visceral, much more about life and death than the anxiety of uncertainty I can sometimes feel.

We quickly gave up trying to find the rig. We did what we should have done as soon as we realized we were lost: pop up to the surface with a safety stop of three minutes at five meters along the way up. (We might have been lost, but we still needed to give our bodies time to off-gas the accumulated nitrogen from the dive and prevent the bends. Getting lost was more than enough drama during this dive.)

At the surface, we saw the oil rig lights not too far away. We maneuvered our gear to float-swim and headed to the rig. We nervously laughed and said we were glad to have found it. But that was it. None of us spoke each other's languages well and didn't feel like having a debriefing on our communication failures.

We all were experienced enough divers to know what we had just done was stupid—and just how lucky we had gotten with the currents. With a slightly stronger oceanic pull or more time passing without us realizing we were lost, we could have surfaced beyond the sight of the oil rig. That would have meant floating all night on the open ocean's surface, hoping daylight would illuminate our location or bring rescuers.

Stars lit up the night sky when we surfaced. My heart was pounding from knowing how easily things could have not gone our way. The anxiety quickly faded into excitement as I looked around at the beauty of the sparkly sky and sea—and remembered all the odd things we had seen underwater.

Part III

RUN

Chapter 7

Loving Running in the Green Mountains

I started running—running meaning the purposeful verb to run versus the joyful sprint, the rushed hurrying, the giggling while you play tag—the summer before eighth grade. For me, the movement created by running engenders different thoughts than those produced on a hike. It might be the same ground you're covering, but it'll feel totally different.

Thoughts on a hike feel more directional and rational. Practical, maybe. You're likely carrying gear and thinking about your food, water, and shelter. Your speed is consistently slow. I notice more about my surroundings on hikes. But I think more widely on runs.

Running feels deeply irrational. Sure, you can pretend there's a point to it. There isn't (except your delight).

As Joyce Carol Oates, the esteemed writer, wrote: "Running! If there's any activity happier, more exhilarating, more nourishing to the imagination, I can't think of what it might be. In running the mind flees with the body, the mysterious efflorescence of language seems to pulse in the brain, in rhythm with our feet and the swinging of our arms."

Running is not a plod from one foot to the other, like hiking. It is a series of small leaps. You have to look closely at a runner to notice the leaps, but they're there. In the sport of race walking, there is a major rule during races: A foot needs to be on the ground at all times. If both your feet are off the ground, you're running, not walking.

You bound from one foot to another on a run. You leap; your thoughts leap with you.

As work and travel have brought me around the world, I've run not just for the endorphins but also to get a better look at where I am. Running is an easy excuse to wander down interesting-looking streets and trails without clear signage. Sure, you could walk the same route. It'd take much longer. Running in a new place lets me quickly ground myself while also exploring unknowns.

It's also just a familiar habit while in new places. I've run around soccer fields in Amazonian villages accessible only by multiple days' travel by riverboat. I've run on trails deep in the Brazilian Atlantic rainforest. On jungled trails underneath troops of howler monkeys in the Petén rainforest of northern Guatemala. On roads around Mussoorie, India, at 6,000 feet with views of the Himalayas stretching into seeming infinity. On small Thai islands where a loop quickly brings you around the entire landmass. On paved circles around parks in Taipei, Taiwan, with many other friendly runners going through the same motions as me.

As so much else changes (as it does if you often travel or never leave home), the constant of putting on some sneakers to head out the door remains the same. Running provides a way to both explore and keep mental stasis.

I started running (and still do) for the pure joy of it. For the love of running. The movement feels good on my body and my brain. Running lets me situate myself in daily good nonsense. It helps when hard thoughts pop up—as they do for all of us.

An easy way for me to accidentally call up a sweaty concept is to look down at my feet and the petroleum-based shoes that cover them. These shoes are different forms of colorful plastic sewn and glued together.

When you wear these contraptions made from fossil fuels, you feel light, strong, and fast. You feel unstoppable. Yet you wear something directly contributing to a phenomenon that will probably stop us all.

For some reason, the act of running helps me touch on these hard topics in a light way. Movement often becomes my way of dealing with sweaty concepts. A concept comes up on its own, you process it as you run (or dive or walk) in a way that is more playful. That lets you think about these sweaty concepts in new ways and not get (as) depressed by them as you would just sitting at a computer.

As the environmental anthropologist Julie Cruikshank wrote in her book *Do Glaciers Listen?*, "Ideas develop in relationship with others and emerge from encounters in particular places at specific times." I cannot separate my intellectual and physical sweating. We craft ideas. It is a bodily process, specific to exact times and places. Ideas themselves might not be alive, but they are not static. We create our ideas in situ. We grapple better with hard topics when we encounter them while moving and playing.

I think we all know this at some intuitive level. Running just happens to be one of the modalities I prefer as a way of getting out of my head and into my body. Others dance, hike, meditate, whatever. The key is just the love part. It's a movement my body loves. I light up on a run. The rhythm feels good to my body, which in turn feels good to my brain. It gives me space to see the magic in the world, not just the horrors. And, for those horrors, it lets me hold them lighter.

Out on a run your mind isn't necessarily there. It's doing the spectacular wander of *whatever* that happens in your brain on pleasant runs. Your mind bounces and dances from subject to subject, often pausing in a cool pool of nothingness, before skipping around to some more thoughts. You visit a thought, smell it like a pretty flower, and then dance around to another idea. Never on purpose, never intentional, never directed—just following your curiosity as your feet follow dirt roads in an Iowa summer as the sun starts its slow meandering descent into a night that'll show thousands of stars reaching across the sky. You'll stretch, shower, eat, and then hang out on a large porch and watch for shooting stars.

After every run, no matter where I run, I come back covered in dirt, messy and tired. Life is tricky like that. Messy, too. Warm showers and being clean after a run is fine. Better is the feeling of being good-tired and covered in dirt. Life is more fun when you're doing things that make you good-tired and dirty.

People think running is a solitary sport. And it is. I spend many hours on my own out on trails. But one of the main joys of my life is running as a social activity. For me, running began as play. Doing it, especially with two of my best friends, Kat and Sophia, was time exclusively reserved for goofing around. We'd run meandering routes around our tiny village, Croton-on-Hudson, where we grew up. We'd giggle, chat, and have only a vague idea of how long we'd been running or our mile paces. Sometimes we'd stop at a friend's house, mid-run, to chat and maybe drink some water.

Every summer in high school, I joyfully ran up and down trails at a running camp in the Green Mountains of Vermont. It was only a week or two, but it was glorious.

There was nothing to do but run twice a day and listen to lectures on running while also goofing around with friends and other kids who love running. As it did with this camp, Nike runs similar camps across the country, often locating them in spectacular trail-running destinations.

The trails in the Green Mountains are perfect for summer running. Made originally for cross-country skiing, they are single tracks that wind thoughtfully through the forest. You run in a line of kids with a few college-age counselors—maybe ten to fifteen people total.

It feels very similar to a hiking group on a single-track path. Ideally the group spaces out a bit but not too much as to become splinter subgroups. That way no one bumps into someone else or steps on the back of anyone's shoes. Hopefully, everyone has enough space to see the upcoming trail. A surprise root, without enough warning, can take down a runner, and then that runner can take down the people in front and behind them. It's like a car pileup but with runners in short-shorts.

The best trails don't take you directly from A to B. They wind, giving you a local's tour of the forest. My memories of these weeks are mostly full of thick green backgrounds and lots of laughter.

It was a lovely paradox—that my most playful running experiences took place at a camp run by Nike, which has dominated the sport of running with its billions earned annually, its questionable treatment of women athletes, and its aggressiveness towards other running companies. It all seems a large mission creep away from the tiny company started for the love of going on a run.

But despite its breeding ground for competitive athletes, those summers felt ridiculous in a good way.

The camp divided up the kids into small running groups by running pace. You knew exactly how much slower you were than all the other campers (and how many might be slower than you).

I never really thought much about it. Sophia and Kat have always been faster runners than me. With them, it's never felt like a ranking thing (as it so easily can with others)—probably because they were never jerks about it. I never thought about our innate running speed abilities on runs with them any more than I thought about how Sophia's hair is curlier than mine and Kat's is blonder—which is to say facts of life that don't have much to do with anything.

Even when Sophia and I did once run the same race—a fun run 10K in our village—we spent a good chunk of it chatting and laughing. It was like any other run, except that at the end we got trophies. Sophia's first place trophy kinda looked like a giant cereal bowl, which delighted us both.

That's what running with my friends has always felt like: fun.

Some of the best parts of the Green Mountains trails weren't even the runs themselves but the lakes and rivers we ended at. You're sweaty and just want to lie down. Better than collapsing on the ground, you get to rush into cold water and splash about. It didn't matter how quickly you had just covered the beautiful trails. Everyone ended at the same place. What mattered was how beautiful the scenery was, how cold and refreshing the lake felt, and how passing the cow pasture on the run smelled terrible.

Soon enough I somehow found myself as a competitive runner. I ran varsity cross-country eighth through twelfth grade on a team with mostly boys (Kat and Sophia went to a different school). As an undergraduate, I attended Grinnell College in Iowa—it's a tiny college full of academic nerds who don't take themselves too seriously. There, I ran on the cross-country and track teams, delighted to have found a DIII school with a huge number of women runners and an enthusiastic coach, Evelyn Freeman, with a strict no-cut, everyone-is-welcome policy.

Cross-country is an odd sport. Unlike the marathon, it is a team sport. You cover a distance (5K in high school, 6K in college), and the placement number of the fastest five runners of each team gets added up. The team with the lowest number wins. You do these races almost weekly throughout a season—same as with track, lacrosse, and the other sports I played in the cross-country off-seasons. Every meet and game seems to matter too much.

Running in a big pack of runners is fun, especially on rural dirt roads where you can spread out, taking up the entire road. Small subgroups form and reform as the miles add up and conversations drift.

Grinnell had plenty of these dirt roads, often lined with rows of corn. A late afternoon early fall run on an Iowan dirt road is one of the best things in the world. It's leisurely and almost too hot. Iowa gets brutally hot in the summer and masochistically cold in the winter. But the in-between times, the few weeks of actual fall and spring meted out by the Midwest, are meteorological perfection.

When running outdoors in an Iowan winter, you don't run but hope with each step to stay upright until the next. When it's this time of year, you don't wait for the early evening—running in the dark on slippery ice is terrifying. You hope your classes are arranged so that you can run earlier in the day, before the darkness hits.

Even if you go on a midday run, your jaw will freeze shut after a certain amount of miles. Your eyelashes get heavy with ice. If I didn't cover my nose with a bandana or something, I'd get a nosebleed—every single stupid run—from the cold, biting air.

A winter run becomes much more dangerous if you stray beyond where you said you'd be. (How can the search party find you when you're limping home with a broken arm, trying to stave off hypothermia, not on the route you said you'd take?)

A summer run is more gentle. It's an outright delight to be savored. You don't have to focus so hard. You can wander—with your steps and your mind. Time stretches out and dances like the summer sunlight that seems to stay almost all night long.

A summer run can be more relaxed, more spiritual of the moment, more following an interesting road. Of course, there's always the risk of a summer thunderstorm, hailstorm, or tornado—which are as scarily dangerous as what can happen on a winter run. Those weather events are the exception. The norm of the late evening summer run is air turning a bit cooler, without ever getting cold, giving you that soft humidity that pets your skin like a favorite blanket.

You don't have to—or want to—pay too close attention to specifics, to details on a summer run. You notice there's corn around you, yes, but at what stage of growth could be anyone's guess.

I spent four years passing by these cornfields almost daily. When is corn harvested? What is its annual life cycle? I have no idea. I vaguely remember certain times of the year when the corn was high and other times the stalks cut down, having been harvested. It was a vague backdrop, always there on my runs but never particularly paid attention to. I didn't need to.

As I ran, my mind wandered from looking at the cornfields to wondering where that corn would eventually be used. I knew these mono-crop fields weren't natural or sustainable. How much diesel, I wondered, went into making those stupid, supposedly compostable spoons?

Notice here I've mostly only told you about cross-country practice. I loved training, even when it was miserable. In high school, racing could be fun at times. I didn't always love it, but sometimes those high school races could be delightfully ridiculous.

One of my high school cross-country coaches did not have the greatest command of time and distance to other places. More than once we'd arrive at a race just after it had started—with enough time to watch everyone run away from us and to eventually catch up to them.

It isn't fun to work hard only to find yourself at the start line everyone else has already departed from. It is fun to pass many people. Chasing a starting line never puts you in a good competitive position. It takes all the pressure off, however. You might as well make a game of it, so we'd count the people passed as we worked our way up to our usual race pack position—the place we might have been had the bus left thirty minutes earlier. Had we left on time the whole thing would have felt a lot more serious, a lot less silly.

A race taken seriously often feels to me like being forced to sit still with a sweaty concept. Racing feels in opposition to play. Where I want to play on a run, the parameters of a race say push and strategize. In a race I can't wander, pause, or get distracted. It feels suffocating. I know the ending already: a finish line where I'm still not good enough, where I could have done better.

Cross-country races in the Northeast are largely private affairs, terrible for the spectators. The racers disappear into the woods and returns twenty-ish minutes later to cross the finish line. The Midwest doesn't have these forests. Instead, races are held on golf courses. You do loops on manufactured grass, within an arm's distance of screaming spectators for the entirety of it. If you could manufacture a hell specific to me, this would be close to it: performing at something where you can always do better, be faster, while strangers scream at you.

The cowbells. The shouts. The faces. All felt inches away from my face as I struggled to maintain my pace and keep my focus on myself. I often accidentally added in unwise sprints to get away from the noise, only to find that it continued the entire race.

I like to run alone or in small groups. I like to think as I run. Running is purely for myself, not for an audience. An audience crowds my brain, adding external pressure. I'm aware of those spectators in a race even when they're not immediately there—like when you pop into the woods on the race's path, leaving the cheering crowd behind.

Racing provides structure, goals, effort measurement, and a deep sense of meaning for many people. I get it. I enjoy winning, moving fast, and trying hard.

But for me, that hasn't ever been the motivator for heading out for a run. A large part of me firmly believes competition flattens the whole point of a run. I'm not trying to race through my existence here. There's so much right here in front of us that is insane, curious, and worthy of our attention.

Sure, the pain of a hard race might turn you inwards to another human place. But the so-called pain cave seems to me to be glorified self-harm and avoidance of this world. In it, runners leave their bodies and the world their bodies currently inhabit. Mile splits too often determine joy or devastation. We all know the concept of time isn't actually real, right?

As racing became more the point of my running, I started getting injured. Being so frequently injured meant I never had a large mileage base from which to do harder workouts because I never had the time to actually get in shape.

Instead I pushed myself too hard, ignoring pretty obvious warning signs from my body to slow down. It increasingly seemed like I was slowing down—or rather, that I was slow. Too slow, too shitty at running to be getting this hurt. Surely, I should be going faster to deserve all this bodily carnage?

It's something I think many of us do—when our bodies scream at us to relax, we panic and push harder. To actually listen to our bodies can feel terrifying. I'm not sure why. Is it that our bodies will tell us something we don't want to hear? A hard truth? That by listening to the calls to slow down, we might then accidentally listen to all of the things our bodies want to say?

I ran myself into a fractured tibia more than once. It requires some pretty serious bodily disassociation to run yourself into broken bones. You can tell it's a fracture and not a shin splint when the point of hurt is singular rather than the entire mass of the shin (and then go get it confirmed by an MRI). It became secondhand nature for me to run my fingers up and down my right shin, feeling to see if the hurt was localizing or if I could ignore it and sneak in some more miles.

I also got misdiagnosed. Doctors tend not to listen to teenage girls and twenty-something women. I was told repeatedly that I must be lying to them about an eating disorder (I wasn't. It's a serious issue faced by many runners of all ages and genders—but just not my issue) or my mileage amounts (again, not lying. I was weirdly getting injuries at relatively modest weekly mileage—not crazy amounts, like 130 miles/week).

Spoilers: I wouldn't find good doctors who listened to me and figured out what was wrong until I moved to California and was thirty. The solution to my right tibia stress fractures is annoyingly simple: properly fitted orthotics.

For years before getting those orthotics, I just felt stupid, like I had somehow fucked up in a way I didn't understand. Everyone else seemed to know how to do running right without constantly hobbling themselves. I cared too much about making it through the respective racing seasons. Worse, I quietly worried that running might not be in my life ten, twenty, forty years from now.

On runs I'd let my mind wander everywhere but my right tibia. Runners are good at tricking their brains. We know tricks to keep our bodies running long miles and for racing—not just to make yourself do better but also to make your opponent do worse.

A basic racing trick: If you're a bit ahead of someone and coming up on a blind curve, sprint your hardest as soon as they can't see you in the turn. When you both come out of the turn, you'll be surprisingly far ahead of them. They won't know that you're trying not to puke from that secret sprint. Instead, if they're not careful, they'll feel demoralized by the unexpected distance between you two, which will accidentally slow their pace for a bit. It's a trick used by all sorts of runners. Meb Keflezighi, an American Olympian, used it near the end of the 2014 Boston Marathon to win, beating Wilson Chebet by a mere eleven seconds.

You can use those racing tactics against your brain. If I run fast enough, my brain can't keep up. It's still there but focused only on getting enough air into my lungs. It's a lousy trick (and a terrible fitness strategy).

I don't think I'm alone in this. I know many other runners who have done this intentionally and even more who do it unconsciously. Other people might use social media, booze, food, or whatever as easy distractions from their brains. Leave it behind. Let it lose. You're trying to win.

It's easy to see a false binary in running: That you can win or not. That there is an obvious and easy binary from which to judge. I sense that this false binary is common in our lives, especially in our thorniest problems, our sweatiest concepts.

Someone will cross a finish line first, yes. But is that a win? Is that the only win? I'm not so sure. I think the concept of winning, of finishing, is squishier than that. It is squishier than we often want it to be.

The messy middle is often uncomfortable. The shades between black and white irk but intrigue me. The lack of tidiness in the gray leaves me feeling unmoored. A shade cannot be absolute. Contingencies always sway it.

The haunting feeling does not disappear, even as I don't race anymore. It lingers. I can smell the fear it brings, asking if you can't ever lose, can you ever win? When do you know if you've won, when you've finished? Will we reach a world after climate change, after problems have been solved, after we've won the big fights? What if those aren't binaries either?

You can lose a race but still have a relationship with running. Likewise, you can cross a finish line first but have lost running. The latter is an unnerving prospect. It hurts, not from the exertion but from loneliness.

You can't possess running or winning. You can lose it, though. What you thought you lost isn't likely to be what disappeared in the loss.

I lost running not in a quick bang but a slow drift. I can't tell you the specific moment I lost running. I know I misplaced it for several years. I'd find pieces and hold on to them with desperation.

By my mid-twenties, it became extremely mentally hard to get myself to run. I found easy excuses not to go on daily runs: being in a country where women don't run, being in a crowded city where you have to stop every block and look for cars coming, being tired, being busy.

Running feels deeply purposeful in its purposelessness. There is not much of a point to running except to run and run the next day—to build a life around the act of running. Even if you're someone who races, those races are mostly an excuse to keep running. There is no end. There are changes, high points and low points. No actual finish line, no tangible purpose except the act itself.

What was it I was desperate for? Endorphins maybe. Or maybe I wanted to cling to the mundane routine of working at something meaningless that turns out to be meaningful. Or the time spent giggling with friends as you run fast and easy miles. Or the quiet mornings with time alone to move about and think as everyone else sleeps.

I used to think the point at which I lost running was when I stopped the physical act of going on runs. I didn't run for a long time.

Once you stop the consistency of daily runs, it becomes harder and harder to keep at running. Not running becomes a feedback loop where you're out of shape, so the run wasn't enjoyable, so you then don't do it the next day. (You're sore! Take a break!) Then I turned around one day and realized I hadn't run in over a year, didn't fully feel myself, and had no desire to head out for a run.

I felt something missing during that time. It pissed me off. Why did others get this running thing and I didn't? I hadn't permanently lost it, of course. I didn't know that then.

Continuing in the same way—miserably plodding along—would not have saved my relationship with running.

For a long time, the sheer existence of running in my life was not enough to make me smile. It had been. Then it wasn't.

I had lost running by then, even as I performed the act almost daily. I needed my mile splits, my racing goals, and my ability (or not) to measure up against other runners.

When I forgot about the love part of running and let the weight of racing slowly crush me, I lost running. It wasn't a clear delineation between having it and not. Instead, it was a slow slip. I'd have it some days, not others. I thought I had lost fitness. What I missed was an almost daily engagement with magic. I had lost the good nonsense of running.

I credit many things to getting running back, but one key thing was this accidental quitting the act of daily runs.

Chapter 8

Retreat in the Santa Monica Mountains

I didn't really run for three years. Instead, I went on occasional hikes. On infrequent early morning swims in over-chlorinated pools. I went to graduate school at Yale's School of the Environment. I went to interesting classes. I hung out with friends. I wrote lots of papers. I read a lot. I got a kidney stone.

Like all of us, I find habits incredibly easy to get out of. I had a test. I had a paper due. I had literally anything else to do than face running.

When stressed I often find that exercise is the first thing to go. It's kinda stupid, really. Exercise (if done smartly) helps reduce stress, helps shake you out of a narrow-brained mindset.

But, living in New Haven and going to graduate school, I only existed in my mind. I forgot about my body. My mind became my entire existence.

At Yale I was surrounded by other people living entirely in their minds and wrestling with many sweaty concepts— all of the time. That brain-only time didn't stop once I left New Haven. I moved to Brooklyn where I felt always on my computer. Always in my brain.

I knew I needed to get running back when I realized I was jealous whenever I saw others running in New York. Even those jogging at stoplights. Or running circles around awful pavement tracks. That jealousy clued me in on the fact that it wasn't fitness I was missing. It was something more ethereal, ineffable, created from a swirling mix of endorphins, exploration, and goofiness. My jealousy had nothing to do with anyone's mile splits or race results. I surprised myself: It turned out I didn't give a damn about that stuff and was equally jealous of the slowest plodding to the most blistering pace of Olympians. I just wanted to run.

I eventually started running again after that break but flailed about. Starting and stopping. I made classic mistakes I knew better than to do but didn't care. (Example: Don't run for a month and then run ten miles. After that, you'll be sore for a while and then won't run again for a few months.)

I started going on runs with Sam, helping him train for a half-marathon. We'd go on runs through Brooklyn, maybe run across a bridge into Manhattan, pick up some bagels, and then take the subway home. It was fun—but only because hanging out with Sam is fun.

The runs themselves were slogs. We didn't live near Prospect Park, so these runs weren't around a single green thing, unless it was trash on the ground or a solitary tree. They were grimy runs, past construction equipment backing up, through run-down neighborhoods and those gentrifying incredibly fast.

The half-marathon was just outside Yellowstone—and opposite our Brooklyn runs. I had signed up for the race with Sam, thinking it'd be a fun goal to force me to run again. It didn't work.

Mere weeks before the race, I stopped running again. The same New Haven excuses (I'm too busy, too tired) applied to Brooklyn. I just couldn't get myself to run those pavement blocks, having to stop at every damn intersection.

As soon as I saw the Tetons and the expansive vistas on our drive, I immediately regretted my lack of fitness. I wanted to explore and run every nook, cranny, high peak, large field, and conifer-forested path. I wanted to play. I wanted to run. I wanted to get covered in dirt, get turned around, and see the same ground-level view from up high.

We camped in Yellowstone for a few days before our race. We'd wake up to picturesque sights: bison casually roaming about, birds flitting above a stream, gorgeous trees, and wide landscapes. Each morning, I couldn't wait to go run.

The day before the race we found a trail for our shakeout run. It's a run that's supposed to be incredibly easy—to keep your legs feeling loose for the next day.

Minutes into the run, it became clear that it would not be an easy trail run—and that it had the potential to be an incredibly fun run. We kept going.

The trail had steep switchbacks, lacing up the side of a mountain. The ground was soft, covered in needles from the trees—some combination of pines, Douglas firs, and junipers. The air smelled amazing. The fermenting trash smell of New York City replaced with crisp air and the aromas of green things. The sky covered in blue and sporadic clouds, not buildings blocking the sun from touching my skin.

Sam, smartly, kept wondering aloud if maybe we should call this run, that maybe it wasn't the best idea for a shakeout run. I kept pleading for just one more curve, one more seeing what's around the bend. I felt more alive than I had in years. More in touch with my body—and just how much it craved playing in these spaces. I didn't want to stop running.

I chickened out when the race showed up the following morning—I ran it but didn't race. The trail run had been incredible, but it didn't get me out of my running rut. If anything, the magic of the trail run hammered home how much I detest racing.

My right knee started hurting during the race and kept hurting for many weeks afterward. I didn't do anything about it. I certainly didn't keep running when we returned to the pavement of Brooklyn.

Despite loving that Yellowstone trail run, I still didn't have running. What I had was a lot of frustration. The trouble was that I knew in theory how to be my own running coach. I understand the logic behind training plans and can write them for others. Following my own is a different story.

To get running back, I needed to take a substantial break to remember why I loved running and return to the act with consistency and compassion. To do that, I couldn't do it alone.

I wanted it to be someone else's fault that *yes, today I have to do this long run.* I needed a team and a coach again. Finding the right fit was surprisingly hard.

The postcollegiate landscape is wide-ranging. You have individuals running marathons. You have elite teams going to the Olympics. You have weekend warriors who treasure their finisher medals and T-shirts. Mostly, it's highly competitive. That didn't fit my newfound approach to running that my jealousy taught me. I wanted something more than a team like the New York Road Runners but one that wasn't just hyper-focused on race results. I wanted the mileage, the occasional hard workouts, the accountability, and the camaraderie of a team without the races—without the competition.

A lot of coaches focus on runners improving their times or beating others. I didn't want to fit myself into that mold anymore. I didn't want my training focused on races I wouldn't compete in. Or, worse, be talked into going back to racing or completing a fastest known time—FKT for short. It's literally what it sounds like: You run a trail and try to cover it as fast as possible, getting the fastest known time for completing it. No thank you. If I trained for anything, it would be for adventures.

When I found Wes Judd he immediately got what I was trying to do with running. Though he is an accomplished competitive ultrarunner, he understood that my priorities were about being a healthy, strong runner whose training celebrations would be big adventures, not races.

I'm picky when it comes to things I care about. If I think you're wrong or not thoughtful enough, I won't listen to you. If I didn't trust Wes or his training philosophy, his coaching wouldn't work for me.

It wasn't so much that I didn't trust my previous coaches—some I did, some I didn't—but rather that their focus misaligned with my own. Theirs were on races and months-long seasons. Mine, even if I didn't always know it, wasn't focused on those things.

Wes got that I loved running as an adventure. I wanted a running life in which my body felt good as my mind played. This is what he designed. The goal of the workouts was to give me structure and tell me what to do—but also to avoid me getting injured and to enjoy my long runs.

We worked together virtually one-on-one, mainly through a Google Docs spreadsheet. One-on-one coaching worked for me—I wanted consistency and enjoyed that the solo runs gave me space for my mind to wander.

Once Wes retired from coaching, I continued training with Candice Schneider, another all-around badass runner. Candice, like Wes, gets what I'm trying to do with running.

Right now, I'm on a team with all the other runners that Candice coaches—even if I don't know most of them because we're scattered around the country. In a lovely, odd way, it also feels like I'm on a running team with every other runner in the world. Running is playful again. I don't hold it so tightly as I once did—even I as prioritize my day's schedule around my run. There isn't a point to my running except to do it and keep doing it. That means I'm not competing against anyone else (even myself). That means we're all on the same side, us runners doing our weird thing.

How I got running back mimics a slightly unexpected source: the bestselling book *How to Do Nothing* by Jenny Odell. She's a multidisciplinary artist writing about how we could best exist as humans in this messy world. Her work often focuses on up-close interactions—the observations of everyday, mundane things and our relationships with them. Her book calls for rethinking how we prioritize productivity while we de-prioritize time in nature and with one another.

Odell writes about the need for retreat and action as well as solitude and engagement with the larger world. This combination of retreat and engagement is her suggestion for how to exist in the world without breaking from the hard things or hiding from them. She suggests times of each. Periods where you are intensely engaged with the larger world and those where you selfishly (in a good way) focus only on yourself.

I didn't know I was following Odell's prescription of how to exist in the world when I was slowly clawing my way back to running, but her suggestions fit well with the mindset that eventually gave me back the joys of running.

When Odell uses the word *retreat*, she does not mean abandoning this world or your hopes for what this world could be. It just means giving yourself a different perspective— standing apart from the problems for a hot second. As she writes, "To stand apart is to look at the world (now) from the point of the view of the world as it could be (the future), with all of the hope and sorrowful contemplation that this entails."

Odell is not the only one suggesting this type of meaningful break as a way to be fully present in the world. Two other authors, Cal Newport and Catherine Price, have written on similar topics from slightly different perspectives. Newport is a Georgetown computer science professor and pop-science writer on focus. Price is a journalist who writes books about fun, vitamins, and breaking up with your phone. Both Newport and Price focus on the steps to disengage from purposely addictive devices, technologies, and entertainment—and fill your life with meaningful activities and connections.

To do so, both suggest putting thought into how you spend your leisure time. All too often we, myself included, relax with whatever activity is easiest at the moment—and usually that's something on our phones. It isn't restorative, though. We don't feel nourished from scrolling on Instagram. We don't feel engaged with mindless internet consumption.

That's partially because it's all brain, no body. Both Newport and Price give explicit, implementable suggestions for how to spend your hours after you rid them of screen time. They urge their readers to replace screen time with in-person relationships and learning non-digital skills. Funnily enough, both recommend learning the guitar.

I'm not saying you should learn the guitar (I prefer wind instruments and non-calloused fingers). But they have a point: Learning the guitar is a different way of learning and moving and being in the world than is Twitter or email. It's a bodily activity. You cannot help but be in the world as you play.

The proliferation of such works points to a genuine need we all have: How do we face the shit of the world without just hiding under our bed covers?

I think this is something we all feel—that's gotta be why there are so many advice columns about climate anxiety. It can be all too easy to doomscroll or write everything off as a disaster not worth engaging in for fear of drowning. It doesn't feel good to see how much of our world looks like a dumpster fire right now. But it also doesn't feel good to hide or assume others will fix everything on our behalf.

It's not just climate change that makes us feel like we wanna hide. Insane politics, school shootings, malnutrition in a world with an overabundance of food, gender violence . . . the list all too easily goes on.

The trick that Odell, Newport, and Price all argue is intentionality. Such intentionality can only come from periods of retreat—of solitude from devices, standing apart from twenty-four-hour news cycles, and purposeful breaks from addictive social media. It lets you rest and better approach the dumpster fires of our world.

Retreat lets you hear yourself. It lets you prioritize yourself.

Now, my running training plan has these moments of both retreat and engagement built into it. Just as I have different runs planned each week, I also have rest days. These rest days, though lacking in the usual endorphins, provide weekly reflections to observe my relationship with running. And, importantly, these movements of retreat are planned. They're not—as they were when I was flailing about—surprise occurrences created from exhaustion or sore quads. They're premeditated.

Rest days help prevent injuries. They also ensure you're running for the right reasons. As Odell writes, "We need distance and time to be functional enough to do or think anything meaningful at all." She's talking about standing apart from society, but it sounds almost like an argument for running rest days.

The same principle underlies both. For you to show up in the world, engage with it, and run in it, you need breaks. Without time and space to evaluate your priorities, you'll chase the wrong things. Without rest, you can't push hard.

You will break if you do not have breaks.

Getting running back, for me, was premised on not ignoring all the hard parts of running but also not forgetting the joys.

That's what we need to do with other sweaty concepts we face: hold space for both the grief and the joy as a mindset to approach the wrestling that sweaty concepts require.

Spending time running outdoors makes it easier for me to hold that space. Now that I have it back, running is a form of retreat for me. As is the physical space where I do that running. My most convenient daily access to nature is on a trail run. Others might find it hiking or ocean swimming or park sitting. We need these physical spaces of retreat to help facilitate our mental and emotional retreats. We cannot engage in good nonsense without them.

When I'm in Los Angeles, a long run in the Santa Monica Mountains always gives me a feeling of disappearing from the world. It helps that you can plan to end your run with a sit on the beach, looking out at the Pacific Ocean where dolphins often pass by.

Dolphins, those strange creatures, are often repositories for our anthropomorphizing tendencies. I know they are for mine. A baby dolphin sighting never fails to make me audibly squeal with delight. Delightful squeals provide the foundation for most conservation work to protect spaces like the Santa Monica Mountains—horrified gasps, too. The divide between good and bad seems clear, except it never is. The beautifully false binary obscures the truth, covering our need to sweat with our questions.

Once on a run in the Santa Monicas, a pair of hikers stopped and asked me where the trail went. I looked at them confused for too many silent moments—I was miles into a long run and tired. It doesn't *go* anywhere. It's 500 miles of dirt paths. Your path is only what you make of it. Sure, you can do a 67-mile point-to-point trip (called the Backbone Trail) across the recreation area—but that isn't necessarily the destination of the trails. You should know that if you're headed out into the wilderness—that there isn't a clear end to this trail. But we expect destinations and finish lines, don't we?

Sometimes a low fog rolls in when I sit on the beach in Los Angeles. Its crisp, wet chill hides the Santa Monica Mountains from me. Those mountains and their massive trail network provide an excellent running playground.

The trails here steeply climb and drop. There are curving switchbacks. The roller-coaster nature of these trails sweeps you along (with some muscled effort, ample water, and tasty snacks).

Other trails in the Los Angeles area can get too narrow for my taste. These are wide. When you're a runner sharing these dirt paths in Southern California with cyclists, it's nice for everyone to have room to avoid potential collisions.

Parts near well-known trailheads can get crowded with runners, hikers, cyclists, dog walkers—and tourists looking to spot a celebrity in the wild. But like most outdoorsy places, you don't have to venture far to be alone.

In a city of almost four million, you can easily run alone on a dirt path that has spectacular views of both mountains and ocean. No one will see you do airplane arms as you sprint downhill, giggling and slightly afraid that you'll trip and tumble down into the steep ravines lining these trails if you don't pick your feet up quickly enough.

The Santa Monicas are a harsh environment—too many people are rescued by helicopter out of these mountains every year. To the untrained eye, they look desert-ish with their scruffy bushes, darting geckos, strange cacti, and shades of brown. Looking closer, you realize the validity of the ecosystem's classification as Mediterranean.

The ocean fog gives a humidity to the area. It isn't always present. When it shows up, it arrives with a surprising density.

When the rains come, everything except the dirt of the trails seemingly turns green. Plants I didn't even know could turn green do. The weirdest flowers show up in the most unexpected places. The side of a cactus will suddenly sprout a flower. The flower, a deep red, won't be pretty but also not ugly. On the ground, tiny purple flowers with an overabundance of delicate petals pop up unexpectedly.

Best of all are the smells. Wild sage and other herbs explode with scents after the rain. The mixture of dirt and these plants creates my favorite aromatherapy. When I go through a scented patch, I slow down and start sniffing deeply, trying to identify what smells so good. It's almost like walking past a restaurant or food cart that smells amazing. It can stop me in my tracks—or at the very least, slow me down, bringing me flying into the exact moment of the present.

Enjoyment often gets a bad rap. It can be seen as self-indulgent and selfish. For too long I internalized the understanding that for something to be meaningful it has to be hard—a bad hard.

We forget about the good hard. You can exert yourself without hating it. It can even be enjoyable. Sometimes I think enjoying things might kinda be the secret to life. It's one of those overly platonic statements—like *love is the answer*—that can be both oh so shallow and deep. *Hey, just relax and enjoy yourself*—it's both the hardest and easiest thing in the world.

Love, joy, play—these things are not antithetical to pushing yourself or getting things done. They're the foundation for a better way of existing in the world. Of finding the good nonsense in life. Of delighting in it.

Many runners walk this fine line of loving what they're doing but also wanting to exert themselves. Some runners like using mantras (I don't—I zone out and daydream). Repeating these phrases reminds those runners why they're doing what they're doing and to remember the right mindset.

Haruki Murakami, the famous magical realism novelist, discusses running mantras in his memoir, *What I Talk About When I Talk About Running*. Murakami comes across a famous Zen saying that many runners use as their mantra: *Pain is inevitable. Suffering is optional.*

Pain might not be as awful as we often assume.

It might also be different from suffering. I didn't understand that for a long time. Not comprehending that distinction led me to ignore the value of pain.

Writer and runner Alex Hutchinson explores the complexity of pain in his book *Endure*. He learns that pain is "a sensation, like vision or touch; it's an emotion, like anger or sadness; and it's also a 'drive state' that compels action, like hunger." And, like those things, pain isn't inherently negative. It paces us, informs us, and lets us strive without exceeding our own limits. Odell's emphasis on balance can also apply to pain.

That balance seems to be the approach so many of these thinkers are pointing out—from the artistic approaches like Odell to the Zen wisdom used by Murakami to the science quoted by Hutchinson. Such balance requires breaks but also showing up consistently to engage.

Running is hard but also easy. Running requires forward momentum. Running asks you to take little steps that add up to miles and miles.

The value of running is almost the same as what Jenny Odell writes: "Sometimes it's good to be stuck in the in-between, even if it's uncomfortable."

How you interact with that uncomfortable pain dictates a lot in our lives. It's no wonder mindfulness meditation has exploded. Pain abounds. We all need ways to navigate it. To acknowledge it, listen to it, but not let it dictate our responses to the world. I've found pain in running to be the same.

Forcing myself to ignore pain completely, I ended up frequently injured. In confusing suffering and pain, I lost the pleasures inherent to being a runner.

Now I don't get stress fractures. Because I'm not grinding myself down, I'm able to go on epic, multi-hour runs on trails in my backyard and around the world. I haven't been injured in years and am now the strongest I've ever been. It's fucking amazing.

The best way I've heard to describe the balance of someone flourishing in a good hard effort is the phrase "fit that looks like grit." (*Fit* here means match with something, like a job or solving a problem in the world—not fitness.) It's from the journalist David Epstein's book *Range: Why Generalists Triumph in a Specialized World*. In it, Epstein argues that having diverse interests and talents (what he calls *range*) is a skill set better suited to today's ever-changing world than overspecialization.

If you haven't read *Range*, you should—it's one of the best accidental self-help (and parenting) research books out there. (Is your child struggling a bit in a class or recently failed a test? Great. Difficult learning makes for better remembering of the subject in the long term, even if it doesn't feel like it in the moment. Acing tests all the time doesn't.)

These generalists often find their paths later in life but thrive when they find them. When they look at problems, they're usually more able to come up with unexpected, creative solutions—and more accurately predict future events (say, will X country invade Y country this year?) than those overspecialized in the academic fields where those problems or predictions lay.

Epstein argues that the same curiosity and lateral thinking that looks inefficient and unfocused on a résumé gives one a better ability to be agile in the strange world we find ourselves in today. That flies directly in the face of how we often picture successful people: someone who knew what they wanted to do at eighteen and, come hell or high water, got it done. Things get tough, they get tougher. Too often we assume those capable of doing extreme or impressive things do so because of their grittiness.

Except that isn't what happens. They can do it because the activity aligns with their specific talents and interests—they have a pronounced *fit* with whatever it is they're doing. If you dig into the data more deeply, as Epstein shows, these people likely found their *fit* after sampling many other careers, skills, and activities. The trick seems to be that they're enjoying whatever it is that they're doing. To reference the Zen quote again: Pain might be present but those truly flourishing—in their *fit*—aren't suffering.

They weren't born knowing exactly what they'd do for the rest of their life. Instead, these successful generalists likely pursued many things and were probably bad at most of them. Looking at them today—in positions of prestige and success— doesn't give you a full picture: You're just seeing them do the stuff that aligns with their skill sets and interests.

If you have too much unthoughtful grit, you might not quit something soon enough. You might miss out on finding your *fit*. Unchecked, I can be gritty to my detriment, bashing my head into the wrong wall instead of pausing to ask if there's not a better way—or if I even enjoy what I'm doing. I think a lot of us are accidentally like this. It feels productive in the moment—and tremendously scary at times to step back and ask some questions. Even scarier would be to quit something that isn't working. But doing those scary things, being honest with ourselves, actually gets us farther in life and in more enjoyable places.

I fixed my running by finding a better *fit*—by finding how I matched with what approach to running. I didn't get running back by doubling down on my grittiness. I run lots of miles not because I am so hardcore but because it gives me tremendous joy. Sure, there's sometimes pain. But I rarely suffer in my runs.

When the *fit* isn't there, I can't do the most basic of things—or if I push through because I feel like I *should*, then my output is shit. When interested in what I'm doing, I can happily do hard, annoying things (and they don't feel so annoying). I know I'm not the only one like this.

Montaigne felt the same way and wrote about it in his singular book, *Les Essais*, published in 1580. Sarah Bakewell explains this tendency of his in her book on Montaigne, *How to Live*: "When he did get an urge to do something, he could apply himself to it with energy. 'I stand up well under hard work; but I do so only if I go to it of my own will, and as much as my desire leads me to it.' He hated exerting himself doing things that bored him."

I think there's a bigger point to be made here: that if each of us went after our *fit* in life, rather than grumpily, grittily doing what we think should be done, we might be much better able to collectively tackle the hard shit in life. We might even have fun.

Most recreation—the best and most enjoyable types— requires good nonsense. A run. A hike. A dive. An interesting book. A delightful conversation. An intriguing movie. They get you going. Your brain is churning, digesting new information, and your body is working. Good nonsense makes you sweat.

Chapter 9

Good Nonsense in Griffith Park

I met a mountain lion once. We didn't exchange names, but I'm pretty sure it was P-22, the lone male mountain lion who inhabited Griffith Park in Los Angeles for a decade. The park is urban wilderness, a slightly oxymoronic term.

On a rainy evening around dusk we both ended up on the same trail, heading in opposite directions. Animals, like us, often prefer trails in the rain. Some animals, like bears, almost always pick paths over bushwhacking, no matter the weather. That can set up some gnarly human-wildlife conflict.

I'm lucky that my brief encounter with P-22 ended without either of us hurt. The almost-dusk light made it hard to see. When I first saw his sleek cat body trotting towards me, my brain tried to make him into a large off-leash dog. I was halfway through the thought of *Where is the owner of this off-leash dog?* when it clicked: *Oh fuck, that's a mountain lion.*

We surprised each other. Both of us stopped at the same time to look at each other. The pause felt like an eternity. It likely wasn't. My brain whirled, pulling out the instructions for a mountain lion encounter: Be large, make noise, and never run away.

I put my hands up above my head. Before I had even started to get the sound out of something (What does one shout in such a situation? *Hello! I am a human! I do not taste like deer!*), he turned left, off the path into the trees and brush.

It was a rare instance of a mountain lion accidentally being seen by a human. They often watch you, completely unseen, until they want to be noticed. Mountain lions usually only want to be noticed when attacking you (a *very* rare occurrence). P-22 hadn't meant to run into me.

I kept telling myself that as I stood on the trail by myself with my hands still above my head. My brain kept looping on the fact that mountain lion attacks are rare while hoping that he hadn't popped into the bushes to side ambush me.

P-22 never reappeared. I kept standing there on the trail, listening hard but mostly just hearing the hum of the nearby highway. Eventually I started slowly walking backward on the trail, my arms still raised, wondering if he was still watching me, unseen in the bushes.

Once I made it to the opening created by an empty parking lot, I put my hands down, turned around, and sprinted home. I got home and locked the door behind me, my adrenaline still spiking.

P-22 never hurt a human. He died in 2022—old, incredibly sick (kidney failure and heart disease), and severely injured (likely by a car) at the age of twelve; he was euthanized by wildlife officials. But as sad as it is that his wildness is lost, there are still mountain lions and even black bears in parts of Los Angeles.

After that day on the trail, afterward, profound awe lingered. I found myself wondering about P-22—how did he spend his days and hours? I kept expecting (hoping, maybe even) to come across him on the trail again. I found a deep sense of excitement (and a tinge of fear) in coming so close to such deep wildness.

Most runs in the park are free of mountain lion encounters. But they're full of interactions with other creatures and humans. One of the best things about the parks of Los Angeles is their sheer diversity—biological and cultural. Everyone and everything seems to use and enjoy these green spaces in a city filled with too much pavement.

Every trip into Griffith is almost guaranteed to remind you of the joy and neighborliness we share with other species. The park cannot help but spark wonder.

Families often spend their weekend mornings hiking in Los Angeles. One time, while I was post-run stretching near my car, a family of five passed me. The youngest boy spotted a lizard. *LIZARD!* he shouted, throwing his arm in the general direction of the tiny creature. I smiled—and feel the same way about lizards. I feel the same way about mountain lions, too.

What Scott Douglas, a prominent running journalist, wrote in his book, *Running Is My Therapy*, feels similar to my feelings towards running that day. He wrote, "What running has done for me for almost four decades, and what I hope it will do the rest of my life, is to help me more often be my best—interested in rather than dismissive of others, engaged in rather than beaten down by work, hopeful rather than fearful toward the future." For me, one of the key things is to be interested in, rather than dismissive of, other creatures in a cosmic way. Running trails seems to be one of the best ways to stumble across and delight in these creatures.

The lizard scuttled away, and the family continued on their walk. My attention shifted from ground creatures to those in the sky. Parrots fly in large groups, chattering loudly, around Los Angeles. For the same reasons I like the parks, like Griffith, they do too. While at least one parrot species (now extinct) used to inhabit North America, it is not these bright green parrots. These parrots are likely descendants of escaped exotic pets.

You hear the parrots before you see them. Their squawks sound harsh against the browns and dusky-greens of the

Mediterranean landscape of Southern California. It isn't the noises most birds make here. Most creatures work hard to blend into the landscape I run through.

I do try to keep an eye out for rattlesnakes on Southern California trails but honestly often forget about them. I trust they'll hear my footsteps way before I see them. One time I saw a small baby-ish rattlesnake on a midday run. It was already scuttling off the path, in fear of me, before I even noticed anything on the trail in front of me was moving.

If I'm lucky on an early morning run as the sun is still waking up, I'll come across coyotes and foxes. Coyotes lounge on grassy spots, which will be filled with picnickers later in the day on a weekend. Foxes pop out from behind bushes and dart across the trails. Sometimes a particularly feisty (and too comfortable around humans) fox will try to follow me for a bit until I turn around and make it clear I'd like to be running solo, thank you very much. Such foxes often remind me of how when you pass parents and small children hiking, the kids will sometimes squeal with delight and start running with you. Both small children and foxes seem to understand the play inherent to a good trail run.

When I run, I rarely look at the ground. I look at the wider landscape and the sky. I watch hawks circle nearby as I climb and descend the rolling hills. I laugh as I run-walk the steeper hills upwards, always amazed that it's a faster way to ascend than a consistent, struggling run. I giggle on the downhills as I pick my feet up quickly, letting gravity do most of the work.

Part of the fun of a Griffith Park run is that it's often full of Californian sunshine. It is bright, joyful, and seemingly ever-present. But that sunshine can get hot, so sometimes I need to find shade to relax within. I think about shade often on my runs in Griffith Park, especially afterward.

Sometimes I run to the park. Sometimes I drive. After one summer run, when I wasn't the one with the car keys, I paced about the car and looked in at the cold water, snack, and clean bra not soaking in sweat. It can quickly get too hot to linger long in direct sunlight during a Los Angeles summer. I meandered back and forth between staring at the water in the car and hiding under a tree's shade, knowing that the keys and their lovely human holders (Sam and one of his best friends, Dodge) would arrive at the car soon enough.

After that run—like all runs in Griffith Park—the heaviness of the dirt hills I'd just run was sinking into my muscles. It is a relaxing feeling, calming with its familiarity. As I stood by the car, watching the family with the little boy excited about lizards, I did a few more quad stretches and toe touches. I know the tightness that follows the heaviness of legs well run. That tightness, unaddressed, can lead to injury.

Other types of tightness cannot be so easily solved. The constriction of my diaphragm. The clench of my jaw. The ache in the sides of my throat just below where the doctor feels your lymph nodes to see if you have strep. When confronted with the scary things of the world, I freak out quietly. I don't scream or shout. I try to clamp down onto something tangible, which (often unhelpfully) is a bodily rigidness. A toe-touch does not so easily unwind these panic displays.

I feel them in familiar unknowns—a dark street. And unfamiliar knowns—glaciers melting, species dying. Sometimes in a forest you can feel the emptiness left behind by the already-extinct. The soon-to-be-extinct can hide well, too. A landscape missing its mammals brings an odd loneliness. You can hear it in Griffith Park. P-22 shouldn't have been by himself. At times I can hear that loneliness even in places like Borneo.

The loneliness of an emptied landscape cannot be drowned out by the gold-mining equipment roaring on the river or the neat rows of palms in plantations. The scream of a landscape's loneliness does not dampen deep in the jungle where trees grow wild and large.

The thick canopy of these trees gives a dark shade. While walking, the slippery mud trails cause lots of sweat to pour down my face. While thinking, the landscape makes me intellectually sweat. Pausing any longer than seven minutes in the shade makes me shiver with cold in the jungle. I shiver with cold after a run in Griffith Park, too, if I wait too long in the forested shade on a hot summer day. Shade is tricky like that.

Too much, I am cold. Too little, I am burnt. I wear sunscreen (most days). It is an oddly mundane choice I make every day: be sticky with sunscreen or risk skin cancer.

It also mimics a thinking habit that I can fall into if I'm not too careful. I have to work hard not to see things as binary—black-and-white thinking, as my wonderful therapist would say. All good or all terrible is a comfortable way of understanding the world. But it lacks nuance—and an understanding of reality.

Because it isn't all black or white. Mostly the world is the squishy middle, the shades of gray, not entirely terrible or great. Sticky sunscreen and skin cancer risk aren't my only options for playing in the sunlight. I could wear fabric woven to protect my skin from the sun. A large smidge of unprotected sun exposure provides health benefits. There's a lot to be found in the middle of a binary.

I don't always think about pretend binaries or sweaty concepts as I run and hike. I weave from shade to sun to shade along the trail. I put one foot in front of the next. Saying that, of course, is as oversimplified as saying I exist.

To have something and then not have it is a loss. It requires the act of having. I don't think you have running. I cannot possess the act of running. That's what running is, right? An act, an action, a state of being, a movement. Could it be something else?

Do we possess mountain lions, like P-22? Do we have foxes? Do we have the climate? Is it something we have and thus can lose?

When I think about possession, my mind usually wanders to an impassioned, off-handed comment made by a conservation colleague of mine. As we floated in a hotel pool in Vietnam, we were discussing the need for better protection in and around a particular conservation area. I wanted a slow and careful discussion with everyone involved. She found my approach tedious, inefficient. (We are friends.) She wanted action and repercussions. "Ugh," she said, "they are eating my animals."

The possessive is a trickster. I cannot possess running any more than my friend can claim ownership over other species. Chat with the right people in a shady situation and you can buy a zebra or even an endangered elephant. But it will never be yours. It can only be its own, if that. It is only part of everything.

Pain can seem overwhelmingly everywhere. The problems scream at me, at us. I wonder why everyone else does not feel this terror. Many do, but why not more?

In those years I lost running, I'm still not always sure what I lost. Sometimes it felt like I lost the future potential of my running and all the unknowns of where running would take me. I felt like a biologist lamenting the destruction of the rainforest. There are hundreds of thousands of species we won't even discover before they are gone forever.

Is that the most important thing to mourn—that we'll never know what was and what could have been? I'm not so sure. Should we care more about the fact that they existed, whether we know about it or not? I'm not so sure those two questions are that different.

That's the most terrifying part about climate change: the looming permanence. We're causing the extinction of creatures that will never again live. We might be causing our end while we're at it. We're certainly causing an extinguishing of a more interesting, diverse world.

We're afraid of losing to climate change. I know I am. It's a beast that threatens to harm everything I love: people, animals, and landscapes. I don't want the sharks to disappear. I enjoy eating many types of bananas.

What we ignore does not disappear. It festers. It continues to grow. Let me be clear: We are killing the earth. We are killing each other. We are suffocating complex life systems with our bullshit. Hiding from this does nothing except harm. Drowning in the sorrow of it does no good. It requires bravery to feel the hurt and still find the heart and the will to play.

Sitting with hard things need not destroy us. Running, when done correctly, teaches us flexibility—to be uncomfortable without switching over into suffering, injuries, and despair. We can practice being uncomfortable on the occasional run and use that skill in our engagement with the larger world. (We also practice being quite comfortable, at ease, and joyful on runs, too.)

Being uncomfortable is not always bad—just as being comfortable is not always good. Novelist, activist, and professor Sarah Schulman understands this. In her 2012 book, *The Gentrification of the Mind*, she writes: "We currently live with a stupefying cultural value that makes being uncomfortable something to be avoided at all costs. Even at the cost of living a false life at the expense of others in an unjust society. We have a concept of happiness that excludes asking uncomfortable questions and saying things that are true but which might make us and others uncomfortable. . . If we want to transform the way we live, we will have to reposition being uncomfortable as a part of life, as part of the process of being a full human being, and as a personal responsibility."

I once saw a turtle die. I was in Komodo, Indonesia, diving where the currents are strong. Cold, strong currents bring in nutrients that big creatures like to eat.

Strong currents are my favorite. Ride them smartly, safely, and calmly, and you'll get whipped around a bustling seascape. The cold water delivered by the currents protects the corals (well enough) against the warming sea temperatures of climate change—at least for now.

It was a hawksbill sea turtle—the ones with a pointy beak that can grow up to 200 pounds. (Think the turtles Crush and

Squirt in *Finding Nemo* that are floating in the open ocean drift lines, relaxing and enjoying life.) Their beak helps these turtles eat sponges growing on corals, even in the small, hard-to-reach spots. Such foraging helps keep corals healthy. But the hawksbill sea turtles are also critically endangered themselves (overhunting and habitat degradation—the usual things that humans do that cause other species to become endangered).

The turtle was around sixty feet down, getting moved about by the currents on a sandy, rocky patch. It wasn't a relaxed, sleeping float. (Turtles sleep a lot. They can sleep underwater and just hold their breath.) Every once in a while it'd jerk and try to move itself. A paddle gesture here and there. But nothing significant. Nothing that actually had oomph.

I could feel that aliveness leave the turtle I watched die. Turtles jolt, paddle, and maneuver around the underwater world awkwardly. They use their four limbs as paddles, scooping and pushing water to place themselves beside food. Turtles move underwater as I imagine I move on top of the water in a kayak: with utilitarian movements and always thinking of food.

The dying turtle had grace—a poetic movement almost. That's what caught my attention. That's what made me stop and watch the turtle. I watched as it eventually stopped making those poetic paddle gestures that had no oomph. I understood what I was watching as the turtle's aliveness diminished. The ocean movements pushed the turtle's body sideways and into a cluster of rocks. It banged, bashed, and floated about sideways, upside down, and right side up—like anything else underwater that is entirely at the whim of the larger ocean movements.

Even though I knew that this was now a corpse of a turtle's body, entering the first step of decomposition to become nutrients for some other, still-alive creature, I hoped I was wrong. I kept hoping maybe it was just a deep sleeper and would wake up, look around, and swim away.

I feel like I'm supposed to tell you I dramatically cried for days for the dead turtle. I didn't. I kept diving for many more days. In the quiet moments aboard the rickety wooden ship I was sleeping on, I'd pause and ask myself: I think I just saw death happen, right? The turtle's death wasn't violent, loud, or sudden. The transition came slowly, happening calmly. There was a beauty in the almost relaxed sigh as life left the turtle.

The calmness confused me. It still does, sometimes. We expect clear markers for death and ends. We anticipate it in our dead turtles as much as we look for it in signs of climate change.

We point to storms and destruction as evidence of change in the levels of atmospheric carbon. We don't see the slow slip. The nuance of what we actually know about climate change gets lost in attempts to get the severity of the situation conveyed to the public. We continue to dumb down how we talk about climate change as we get more desperate for general awareness of the problem—and wait for that awareness to create tangible solutions.

It's not that we don't know climate change is happening. It for sure is. Too often, what is being lost in the story of climate change are all the slow drips of changes happening— and likely to happen. Increasing nighttime temperatures, shifts in rainfall, and bird migration tweaks aren't as dramatic as hurricanes, wildfires, and the other clear markers of life-altering bad changes. It makes sense they aren't covered as dramatically—the slow slip is, honestly, a boring narrative. And yet, most of climate change will not come as Armageddon. The destruction is mostly going to come in the form of small background changes in patterns we rarely even notice now.

We act as if despair will bring us to a better world. As if ignoring sweaty concepts will make the problems answerable. It won't. I understand the sadness, angst, and anger of knowing climate change science and watching the ineptitude, the inaction, the lack of real solutions.

As Sara Ahmed writes in *Living a Feminist Life*, "But what else do we avoid if we avoid confrontation?" We avoid discomfort, feeling tired, and hard effort. But we also avoid living with our own thoughts, being present. We avoid joy, engagement, and living life fully.

I messily flail around in the enormity of my feelings about climate change. These problems are messy and will not be neatly solved. Pretending otherwise does not help. It hurts.

What are we afraid of when we think about climate change and extinction? A big part of it, I think, is loneliness. These other species are our neighbors and sometimes even our friends.

Extinction can feel like the loneliness you'd experience if everyone left your neighborhood, even if you didn't know them. We humans have an innate capacity to feel like animals are our companions in life. Some annoying. Some precocious.

Cockroaches can be somewhat cute. Once I lived on a jungled island in remote Indonesia doing climate change research. I did not know the language fluently and felt lonely often. A tiny cockroach lived in my sink's drainpipe. Her face was a calming sight.

All my days were spent talking about problems: rainfall changes, floods, droughts, trees dying, and crop harvests failing. Problems I could see no immediate answer to. I learned more each day about the complexities of these specific climate change problems in a language I could not fully understand. I felt silly and sad.

The tiny cockroach did not know these problems. She'd crawl up into the sink from her drainpipe and twitch her antennae at me. We'd look at each other. I would be covered in stress sweat and humid jungle-induced moisture. I doubt she ever was.

I know the other humans who lived on that island with me had stress sweat. They were hyper-aware of climate change, of what the looming apocalypse meant for their way of life and their grandchildren.

Part of the reason I felt so lonely was that no one even close to my age lived near me. Parents and grandparents had worked hard to get their adult children out and away from this beautiful island. Other adults and small children remained. They farmed their crops, tended to their animals, and worried.

It is a story repeatedly told. The location is usually the starkest change. The message stays consistent: The monster of climate change caused by the Haves is coming to destroy the Have-Nots. Eventually it might even destroy the Haves. We all will lose. Some will lose worse than others.

My throat hurts. It tightens with anxiety. I clench my jaw when I hear these overly simplistic narratives. We've already lost if these are the dominant stories we tell about climate change. We return to the binary. We return to an avoidance of sweaty concepts.

It becomes easy to glob onto other binaries—good/bad, poor/rich, those with agency/those without. Such binaries obscure. They detract from valid criticism. They strip people of their humanness. These binaries can be very true, but they're also not the entire story. Painting the Have-Nots as static figures who can only ever be victims strips people of their agency and ability to solve problems (even if most of those problems were very much created by the Haves). And, it lets the Haves pretend as if they'll never be impacted by climate change.

Such a telling writes the ending to a story not yet finished. Climate change or any of the other problems threatening to dismantle society do not need to destroy us all—and destroy some worse than others. We can write other stories. There is still time. Forcing a binary onto our worldviews lets us forget we don't have to despair. That's why good nonsense is so important.

Sometimes I wonder if others have learned a dance I don't yet know, a dance that lets you feel the pain and the joy? I don't know. I think I might be learning the steps to that dance, though. I think the more I adventure, the more I dance.

I used to try to outrun sweaty concepts. I liked asking questions to other people—as if they had access to secret information I did not. I didn't like being stuck with just these bold questions and me.

Exercise- and adventure-induced sweat differs from the stress sweat induced by the existential anxiety of losing to climate change or income inequality or the AI Pandora's box or ocean acidification or the million other sweaty concepts my brain can queue up in a second. The latter type of sweat smells rank. Worse than a shirt sweated into for weeks, unwashed on a backcountry hike.

Dealing with sweaty concepts is much better than despairing. A sweaty concept doesn't mean we ruminate forever. It, instead, gives us the strength to fight for a better world. It creates a mindset of engagement, even as we know individual actions alone won't fix the colossal problems of our world. You alone will likely make no meaningful impact on the planet. Your carbon footprint pales compared to the mega-corporations. Your individual plastic straw usage makes no difference to the overall sea turtle population. Yet nothing has ever happened except by the actions of individuals who gave a damn.

I think we need to reexamine how we think of leadership and engagement with the world. We need more good nonsense in both. For me, that means doing things in your own style. It is a celebration of your own capacity to guide your life.

I do not mean some libertarian bullshit, of no taxes, no helping others, of not understanding a rising tide lifts all boats. Instead, I mean an understanding that we're all in this together. We can depend on one another while celebrating our individuality.

It's easy to give the world the middle finger, be pissed off about all the problems and decide that all the problems are too big and too many—and go hide under your covers or binge Netflix or scroll Instagram. The problem is, though, that it's a lot more fun to give a damn.

It's more interesting to be engaged in life—the good and the hard.

Leadership in your own style requires doing what thrills us, excites us, not what we think we must do. You care deeply about sports bras for teenage girls so that they don't quit playing sports? Great. Go get after that. You want better trail access in predominately Black communities? Wonderful. Make it happen. You keep noticing that the local duck pond is kinda gross and someone really should deal with it? Perfect. Start figuring out how you contribute.

I'm not talking about writing a big check or signing a petition, although those are sometimes helpful. Instead, I want you to get after what lights you up. What drives you. You don't have to solve everything everywhere, but you do have to care. Sweaty concepts won't let you not care—they'll come after you whether you want them to or not.

Get involved. Make friends. Crack jokes. Face hard problems together. Show up in a way that feels good to you.

It's not about only doing the hard things. An engaged life requires giving yourself plenty of time in nature and moving your body—and enjoying both. Seeing things through a lens of good nonsense lets you not drown in the hard shit of life. It takes you to a mindset where you can still work on the big problems and keep having fun. Because life is all about fun and joy and play.

That play lets you hold things less tightly. You're still holding them. But in a lighter, looser way. I'm not sure why, but somehow there's a magic in that light touch.

A better world comes from play, not shame. We do not solve climate change—or tackle any sweaty concepts—by berating ourselves. We work towards the world we want by actively cultivating wonder and joy. It is these things that lead to good solutions.

Solutions can come from shame, but they are not the ones we want. We want to create a better world. That creation requires imagination and play. It requires lightness and silliness. Shame destroys all that.

Play requires seeing the calamities of the world but also the joy. Moving my body in beautiful nature helps me remember that joy while working through my thoughts and feelings about the calamities. It lets me think with my brain and my body. I better engage with the world during and after such adventures.

Such engagement may not always be comfortable. That doesn't mean it won't also be joyful. We get agency and bravery from asking bold questions.

I started this book by saying I don't have answers. I still don't have any to give you. Instead, all I've got is a hunch that we should be sitting with these sweaty concepts a bit more than we usually want to—and that a better way to be with them is moving our bodies by playing in nature.

We all feel lost and confused and overwhelmed at times. It makes sense. Some of the shit we're up against is big and gnarly. We find our own agency in this world when we give ourselves permission for all of the feelings—good and bad. In that way we're able to celebrate it all. We can engage with the hard stuff—and the good stuff. We need the grief as well as the joy.

But, really, we do need that joy. We need the good nonsense.

Engaging with sweaty concepts helps us have happier lives. To both retreat and engage. To value our leisure, our joy, our play. To hike, to dive, and to run. To hold space for the hard, shitty things in the world without breaking.

Acknowledgments

Life, like writing and running, is a team sport. I'm lucky to be on a team with some amazing friends, family, mentors, and colleagues.

This book would not exist without Elizabeth Allen. Elizabeth, thank you so much for all your help, guidance, and edits. Without you, this book would just be a pile of notes I was pretty sure might have the potential to be a book.

This book wouldn't have been published without the work of three talented individuals: graphic designer Cyrus Hernstadt, copy editor Elissa Curcio, and book designer Sarah Lahay. Thank you all so much for the fantastic work you did. Working with you has been a delight.

Wes Judd and Candice Schneider: Thank you for coaching me in running. Running is so much fun, and working with each of you has ensured it is fun.

Kat and Sophia: You guys are the best. I've known that since day one of meeting you both—and I continue to count my lucky stars that I get to call you both close friends. Thanks for always being down to goof around with me—on a run or wherever.

Michael Dove and Fred Strebeigh: Thank you for being such great professors and always being willing to write me a letter of recommendation, to suggest a book I should read, or to tell me you think I can do whatever harebrained academic scheme I've dreamed up. I'm sure you'll each notice your academic influence throughout this book.

David Campbell, John Whittaker, and Brigittine French: Thank you for being such excellent professors in college and for helping me so much afterward. Without your influence, I certainly wouldn't be doing what I'm doing today. You, too, will notice your academic fingerprints throughout this book. I really appreciate it.

Friends and Family: I'm lucky enough that there's a fairly large number of you I want to thank for being the best people ever. I'm nervous that I'll space on someone, so as cool as it is to see your name in a book, I'm not going to do that. Instead, if you're like, huh, I think I count here—you do. You're the best. Let's hang out soon.

Dad: You'll find many of our overlapping interests in this book: adventure, books, and overthinking both adventure and books. Thanks for being the world's best Dad.

Mom: I miss you very much. I think you'd be both proud of this book and a bit terrified of some of the stories within it that I purposely forgot to tell you. (I promise I'm usually careful when scuba diving.)

Fiona: You're the best little sister I could ever have. I'm so glad you exist. Hanging out with you is the best.

Sam: I'm so lucky I met you. I'm even luckier that we get to spend our life (and days) being goofballs together. Thanks for always being willing to pull leeches off of me and to know where to find delicious meals in cities around the world. Adventuring with you (big and small) is a true delight.

About the Author

Sarah Austin Casson is an environmental anthropologist, a job that has brought her all over the world. She has worked with farmers, wilderness rangers, policymakers, scientists, and a bunch more people to look at some of our gnarliest problems: climate change, collapsed prehistoric societies, wilderness conservation, and others. She's interested in how we interact with one another and the natural environment, how we conceptualize our worlds, and what it means to exist in the nuances our world demands. You'll find her eating delicious food in dense cities and goofing around in remote wildernesses. She's climbed volcanoes, summited mountains, dived deep into the oceans, and traversed jungles.

Numerous grants and awards have funded Sarah's work. These include the Yale Law School's Global Justice Fellowship, Tropical Resources Institute Endowment Fellowship, Council on Southeast Asia Studies Research Grant, Carpenter-Sperry

Research Fund, Charles Kao Research Fund, and many others. Her writing has been published in many trade and academic locations. Sarah is an associate member of the Society of Environmental Journalists and a Fellow of the International League of Conservation Writers. She studied at Grinnell College (BA Anthropology) and Yale University School of the Environment (MESc).

She can be found online at:
SarahAustinCasson.com